Understanding
Jehovah's
Witnesses

Understanding Jehovah's Witnesses

Why They Read the Bible the Way They Do

Robert M. Bowman, Jr.

BAKER BOOK HOUSE
Grand Rapids, Michigan 49516

Library of Congress Cataloging-in-Publication Data

Bowman, Robert M.
    Understanding Jehovah's Witnesses: why they read the Bible the way they do
/ Robert M. Bowman, Jr.
      p. cm.
    Includes bibliographical references.
    ISBN 0–8010–0995–2
    1. Jehovah's Witnesses—Doctrines. 2. Bible—Criticism, interpretation,
etc.—History. I. Title.
BX8526.B674 1991
289.9'2—dc20   91-3034
                                               CIP

Contents

84197

Preface

Uh . . . is this one of those "anti-Witness" books? Jehovah's Witnesses aren't supposed to read such things. And besides, aren't there already a lot of books that criticize the Jehovah's Witnesses? If this is one of those, why do we need another?

Good questions. Actually, this is not really an "anti-Witness" book. I am not an ex-Jehovah's Witness (and therefore am not an "apostate") and am not writing this book to tear down the Witnesses. The focus of this book is on understanding Jehovah's Witnesses, not attacking them. In fact, the first two chapters do not criticize the Jehovah's Witnesses at all, and even the rest of the book is more concerned with understanding the Witnesses than with criticizing them. In a sense, I have written the book more for orthodox Christians than for Jehovah's Witnesses. I have tried to help Christians understand the Witnesses better and show that we can learn positive lessons from considering the ways in which Jehovah's Witnesses read the Bible. Of course, I do hope that Jehovah's Witnesses will read the book, too.

One of the nice things about a book is that you can stop reading it at any point. I encourage you who are Jehovah's Witnesses and unsure whether you ought to read this book to try reading to the end of the second chapter. I don't think you'll find anything that offends you, and you may even be pleasantly surprised to find much with which you can agree. Having read that far, you can then decide whether to read more; and again, you can always stop.

This is also an unusual book about Jehovah's Witnesses in that, although I am an evangelical Christian (what Witnesses call a "born-again"), I frequently point out errors into which we evangelicals all too often fall. Evangelicals are not better people than Jehovah's Witnesses. I do think evangelicals have the truth, and not Jehovah's Witnesses, but I do not think this is because evangelicals are better, stronger, smarter, more sincere, more dedicated, or even more "spiritual" (though of course I do believe that God's Spirit must open our minds to see and believe God's truth).

I have also departed from the practice of some writers of regarding Jehovah's Witnesses as unfortunate and innocent dupes of a sinister organization that practices brainwashing. Instead, I hold Jehovah's Witnesses as responsible for their beliefs as are evangelicals or anyone else. This does not mean that I am not critical of the Witnesses' organization, but it does mean that I focus more on Jehovah's Witnesses as people and less on their function as representatives of their organization. Again, my interest here is in helping Christians understand Jehovah's Witnesses better, not in simply attacking them or their organization.

One of the most loving things anyone can do for other human beings is to speak the truth to them even at the risk of being rejected. However, it is all too easy for those who think they have the truth (and this goes for both evangelicals and Jehovah's Witnesses) to be so caught up in asserting that their beliefs are "the truth" that they run right over the people they are supposedly trying to help. The truth will offend those who are committed to falsehood, but we need to make sure that it is *the truth* which offends them, not our offensive manner of presenting the truth. In this book my goal is to "speak the truth in love" (Eph. 4:15). Since both my knowledge of the truth and my practice of love are imperfect, I am open to correction on both counts; but as God is my witness, this has been my goal.

Several persons have read this book in manuscript form

and have made valuable suggestions and insightful criticisms. I am grateful to Elliot Miller, editor of the *Christian Research Journal*, for permission to use expanded versions of four articles of mine from that periodical as chapters in this book, and for his editorial contributions to those chapters. Thanks go to the rest of the research staff of the Christian Research Institute, especially Ken Samples and Jerry and Marian Bodine, for the many helpful discussions we have had on the subjects treated in this book. I also had helpful critiques from persons associated with other ministries: James Earl Stewart of Answers in Action; Duane Magnani of Witness, Inc.; Randall Watters of Bethel Ministries; David Reed of Comments from the Friends; and Richard Fisher of Personal Freedom Outreach. Dr. Vern S. Poythress of Westminster Theological Seminary in Philadelphia read and critiqued an earlier draft of this book, and his thinking on the personal and social factors in biblical interpretation have strongly influenced the approach I take in this book. These friends of mine have differing perspectives on some of the matters covered in the book, and I have tried to learn from all of them. Of course, I take sole and final responsibility for its contents.

The purpose of this book is more fully explained in the introduction. Here let me say that I intend this book to be a means of opening up dialogue with Jehovah's Witnesses about the Bible. If anyone wishes to pursue such dialogue with me, they may write to me at the Christian Research Institute, P. O. Box 500, San Juan Capistrano, CA 92693–0500.

Introduction

J ehovah's Witnesses consider themselves followers of the teachings of the Bible. They insist that they recognize the Bible as the only infallible guide to truth. They accept the same sixty-six books of the Bible as do Protestants. And they defend an understanding of the Bible's inspiration and infallibility that is strikingly similar to that held by evangelicals. (By the way, for those Jehovah's Witnesses unfamiliar with the term, *evangelicals* are Protestants who hold to the Trinity and salvation by grace alone through faith in Christ on the basis of the Bible as the infallible word of God.) For instance, Jehovah's Witnesses could assent to practically everything (with perhaps some reinterpretation) in the Chicago Statement on Biblical Inerrancy except its trinitarianism and its emphasis on the centrality of Christ.[1] Yet their doctrines are so consistently contrary to evangelical theology that one evangelical has dubbed them "apostles of denial."[2]

How is it that Jehovah's Witnesses seem to agree with evangelicals so closely on the authority of biblical doctrine yet disagree so markedly with them on the substance of biblical doctrine? In this book I shall address this question broadly in terms of the hermeneutics of Jehovah's Witnesses.

What Is Hermeneutics?

The term *hermeneutics* can be understood both prescrip-tively (as concerning what ought to be done) and descrip-tively (as concerning what in fact is done). Prescriptively hermeneutics is "the study of those principles which should guide our interpretation," in this case specifically our inter-pretation of the Bible.[3] Descriptively hermeneutics may be understood as the study of the presuppositions, attitudes, social influences and conscious principles that contribute to one's interpretation of the Bible.

In one sense it is impossible to read the Bible or anything else without bringing to one's reading a whole constellation of presuppositions and attitudes, influences, and principles. These may be either good or bad. Presupposing that truth is one, or having a humble attitude about one's ability to under-stand God's truth, is good. Presupposing that there is no one truth, or proudly expecting to comprehend God's truth per-fectly, is bad.

The task of hermeneutics, then, can be conceived as having two stages, the first descriptive and the second prescriptive. It begins with identifying those presuppositions, attitudes, influences, and principles that contribute to interpretation. This first stage is preparatory for the second, that of sorting out appropriate from inappropriate presuppositions and atti-tudes, constructive from destructive social influences, sound from unsound interpretive principles.

The descriptive stage of hermeneutics may be further sub-divided into two parts. The first concerns what leads a per-son to adopt a belief or set of beliefs initially, whereas the second concerns what serves to maintain a person in those beliefs.

Goals of This Book

My purpose in this book is to offer a hermeneutical analysis of the Jehovah's Witnesses' interpretation of the Bible. I hope to help evangelicals better understand Jehovah's Witnesses and also to help Jehovah's Witnesses better understand themselves. To evangelicals I issue a challenge to be more understanding and compassionate in their encounters with Jehovah's Witnesses and to learn both positively and negatively from the strengths and weaknesses of the Jehovah's Witnesses' approach to the Bible. To Jehovah's Witnesses I issue a challenge to be more aware of the unexpressed factors and influences that contribute to their distinctive interpretations of the Bible and to examine afresh the foundation on which those interpretations rest.

The plan of this book is as follows. Chapter 1 offers a positive statement of what ought to be the guiding principles of biblical interpretation. Here I cite statements of these principles from Watchtower publications to show that, at least in theory, Jehovah's Witnesses recognize the validity of most or all of these principles. From this chapter it will be clear, I hope, that my intention is not to tear down Jehovah's Witnesses as people, nor to turn them away from the Bible (anything but). Since this chapter does not challenge any of the Jehovah's Witnesses' doctrinal beliefs, Jehovah's Witnesses who wish to avoid reading "anti-Witness" literature may want to read that chapter before deciding whether to read the rest of the book.

Chapters 2–4 present a discussion of those factors which evangelicals and Jehovah's Witnesses both cite (from different perspectives) to explain why they differ on the Bible's teachings despite their apparent agreement on the inspiration and authority of the Bible. Here I will show that these factors are indeed significant and argue that Jehovah's Witnesses are hindered from understanding the Bible correctly, especially because of their views on religious authority (chapter 3) and the use of their New World Translation (chapter 4). (A discussion of alleged scholarly endorsements of the New World Translation is found in Appendix A.) I will also show, no doubt to the surprise of both evangelicals and Jehovah's Witnesses, that these factors are inadequate to explain why the Witnesses adopt their beliefs in the first place rather than those of evangelicals.

Chapter 5 is a historical and theological analysis of the foundational presupposition underlying the Jehovah's Witnesses' belief system. Here I will show that this foundational presupposition is unbiblical, that it is not at all unique to Jehovah's Witnesses, and therefore that it is the way Jehovah's Witnesses apply this presupposition to their study of Scripture that results in their distinctive doctrinal system.

Chapter 6 presents an overview of those specific factors which draw people to the Jehovah's Witnesses' beliefs and those which reinforce them in those beliefs. In this chapter I will discuss both doctrinal and nondoctrinal factors and explain how the doctrinal and nondoctrinal are much more closely related than is commonly realized. I will explain why these factors discourage Jehovah's Witnesses from gaining a proper understanding of the Bible.

In chapters 7–8 I will move from the theoretical to the more practical by looking at Jehovah's Witness interpretation of the Bible in action. In chapter 7 I will focus on one verse of the Bible (Luke 23:43), consider the arguments the Jehovah's Witnesses adduce in favor of their interpretation, and draw attention to the various hermeneutical factors that contribute to their interpretation of that text. Additional examples of Jehovah's Witness interpretation will also be given. In the process I will show how these factors relate to their foundational presupposition discussed in chapter 5. In chapter 8 I will discuss a major theme in the Bible (the divine name), again interacting with the Jehovah's Witnesses' interpretation of the Bible on this matter. This last chapter is especially important, because it shows that the way Jehovah's Witnesses read and interpret the Bible has consequences for their perception of the "big picture" in Scripture. Appendix B presents a short word study on the Greek word *stauros* (which the Witnesses say should be translated "stake" rather than "cross") as a case study in the interpretation of single words.

Limitations of This Book

Finally, a word about the limitations of this book. The hermeneutical foundations of a religious group is such a broad topic that it is impossible to lay out all of the evidence pertaining to every point I make. This study provides a broad perspective on an incalculable number of facts. An exhaustive study would include reference to the thousands of instances of interpretive choices made in Jehovah's Witnesses' literature and the arguments they present in favor of those interpretations. This book makes no pretensions to such exhaustive detail. Where I have made assertions that I anticipate will be questioned, I have given examples or made reference to other works which more fully explore and document my assertions. Such documentary references have, however, been kept to a minimum. This book should be treated as an overview and introduction to an evangelical appraisal of the foundations of Jehovah's Witness hermeneutics, not as a definitive response to Jehovah's Witness beliefs.

1

Approaching
the Bible
in Dialogue

Evangelical Christians and Jehovah's Witnesses often engage in dialogue concerning their doctrinal differences, yet to no avail. Such dialogue can have a greater chance of success if both sides will first agree to abide by certain principles of truth-seeking. This may be thought of as establishing "common ground," as long as it is understood that such common ground must itself be an approach to truth that honors God. In fact, it is inevitable that even such common principles will be understood and applied differently by evangelicals and Jehovah's Witnesses. How this works out in practice is really the point of this book.

Establishing common ground, then, will not guarantee eventual agreement but will increase the chances of mutual understanding and of the discovery of truth. Discussing biblical truth is likely to be unproductive unless all who are involved at least tacitly agree to most or all of these principles.

In the view of some evangelicals, committed Jehovah's Witnesses will not agree to these principles, so they regard discussing biblical truth with Jehovah's Witnesses as a waste of time. However, in my view the difficulty is not in getting a Jehovah's Witness to agree to these principles. My concern is that I do not see Jehovah's Witnesses consistently *following* or *applying* these principles. But then, to be honest, we evangelicals often fall short of consistently applying these principles, too. We may have the truth (I am convinced that we do), but that does not mean that we understand the truth infallibly or that we interpret Scripture infallibly.

Thus, if we are to be honest, we should not approach Jehovah's Witnesses with the attitude that we are better interpreters of the Bible than they are (although overall our interpretation of the biblical teaching is true and theirs, we are convinced, is not), as if somehow we are simply smarter or better informed. Rather, we should humbly but confidently approach Witnesses with the attitude that we all need to grow in our understanding of the Bible, but also with the conviction that the evangelical interpretation of the Bible is essentially correct.

Throughout this chapter I refer to statements in the publications of Jehovah's Witnesses that acknowledge the validity of these principles. The purpose of these citations is simply to remind Jehovah's Witnesses that these principles are things they already believe, or at least that their writers say they *should* believe. Again, these are principles which truth-loving people should have no great difficulty admitting to be valid, once they consider the facts in the matter. Thus, in the end what will really make the difference is not how smart we are, or how much we know, but whether we love the truth above all else.

The Truth of the Bible

Many radically different religious groups today profess to believe that the Bible is true, that it is the word of God. But what does it *mean* to say that the Bible is God's word? It is vital that we understand the implications of this confession and obtain agreement as to its significance if we are to discuss the Bible's teachings with others.

What follows, then, are some indispensable principles that spell out in detail the significance of confessing the inspired truth of the Bible. If you try to enter into dialogue with people who say they believe the Bible is the word of God but do not adhere to these principles, you should recognize that they either have a different Bible or a different idea of what it means for the Bible to be God's word.

The Inerrancy of the Bible

The Bible, as the word of God, is inerrant, or without error (Matt. 5:17–18; John 10:35; 2 Tim. 3:16). Any teaching, then, that denies or undermines biblical inerrancy is to be rejected. It is double talk to call the Bible God's word and then to charge it with error.

Jehovah's Witnesses certainly need no convincing on this point. Their books are filled with references to the Bible as the inspired word of God and defend the Bible as without error of any kind. For example, the book *You Can Live Forever in Paradise on Earth* states, "Yet the Bible does not contain only true history. *Everything* it says is true."[1]

The Authority of the Bible

The Bible is the standard by which all human teachings, even of God's people in leadership, are to be tested (Acts 17:11; Gal. 1:8). While the opinions of human beings may be valuable aids in understanding the Bible they can never be the standard by which the meaning of the Bible is determined, nor can their teaching be regarded as indispensable to gaining the knowledge of the truth (1 John 2:20). Otherwise those people, not the Bible, become the supreme authority.

In theory the Jehovah's Witnesses recognize the validity of this principle. For example, *You Can Live Forever in Paradise on Earth* warns, "But what if the teachings of the religious organization with which you are associating are not in harmony with those of God's Word? Then you have a serious prob-

lem. It is the problem of deciding whether to accept the truthfulness of the Bible or to reject it in favor of teachings that the
Bible does not support."[2] However, in practice they are willing to apply this test to any religion other than their own. They
believe it would be wrong for them to doubt the teachings of
their leaders.

Because this point is so troublesome, I will devote a full
chapter to it later in this book (chapter 3). Here let me simply
emphasize what can be agreed on in advance. We should have
no trouble agreeing that a person who is *outside* of a particular religious organization must first compare its teachings
with those of the Bible *before* accepting that organization as
having any authority or claim to truth. For example, presumably no one ever becomes a Jehovah's Witness by first accepting without question that the Watchtower leadership's teaching is directed by God and *then* accepting on that basis the
Jehovah's Witnesses' beliefs about God, Christ, salvation, the
kingdom, and the rest. Rather, people convert to the Jehovah's
Witnesses' beliefs because they are somehow convinced that
they are as a whole taught in the Bible, and then allow the organization to govern their thinking on specifics.

Moreover, once the believer examines a religious organization's claim to teach truth, accepts it as valid, and places
some measure of confidence in the organization's teaching, he
or she should recognize that no human organization is infallible. We should also all be able to agree that the teachings of
any organization, no matter how authoritative it is, must
cohere with the Bible or it is in error. Again, the Jehovah's
Witnesses agree that their organization is not infallible. They
acknowledge those mistakes which the organization itself has
admitted in its publications, and no others, but at least they
do admit that the organization is not infallible.

Finally, even though Jehovah's Witnesses may find the idea
inconceivable, they will almost always agree that *if* there
were a conflict between their beliefs and the teachings of the
Bible, their own beliefs would have to be judged in error.
They do agree that the Bible is in this sense the final word on
any subject.

If we can agree on these things, it is possible to discuss the teachings of the Bible with one another, despite our disagreements about the authority of religious leaders.

The Clarity of the Bible

Since God wishes his word to be understood by all who seek the truth, the Bible must be assumed to be clear. The alternative is to regard the Bible as an esoteric book that can only be understood by a priestly caste or ecclesiastical elite. Human teachings cannot be evaluated by truth-seekers on the basis of the Bible if the Bible is written in a spiritual code known only to initiates. Since the Bible is to be used to evaluate the teachings of even godly men entrusted with special authority (Acts 17:11), we conclude that the Bible is clear enough to be understood by any truth-seeker, apart from the authoritative teaching of any religious organization.

Again, the Jehovah's Witnesses agree that the Bible is written to be understood and not in some cryptic code only a spiritual elite can understand. For example, a recent Watchtower book speaks of "the plain teachings of the Scriptures."[3] It is true that the Watchtower also teaches that the Bible is written directly for the "anointed" and that the "great crowd" must gain their understanding of the Bible from the "anointed." However, it is also true that the Jehovah's Witnesses are taught that the meaning of the Bible is "plain" enough that it can be shown to those in the "great crowd" directly from the Bible itself. Thus, at least in principle, the Witnesses believe that the Bible is written in plain language meant to be understandable to common people.

The Necessity of Careful Study

It is possible to overemphasize the clarity of the Bible and in so doing fail to recognize that the Bible is not always simple or easy to understand. Peter stated explicitly that some things in Paul's letters are hard to understand (2 Peter 3:16), and this applies to other portions of God's word as well (Dan. 12:8–9). Nor should this fact be surprising, since the Bible talks about God and our relationship to him—not an easy sub-ject. The essential truths of the Bible are clear enough for the simple-minded to recognize and believe if they are willing, but not so obvious and simple that they cannot be twisted by false teachers (2 Peter 3:16; 1 Tim. 1:7). This means that to under-stand the Bible fully, and especially to refute false teaching, careful study is necessary (2 Tim. 2:15). Those who complain that Christian doctrine is too difficult to understand ("Why would God make it so complicated?" is their usual cry) wrongly assume that truth is something God "makes up," instead of something real about God and his relationship to us.

Although Jehovah's Witnesses tend to view the Bible as less complex than do evangelicals, they would agree that the Bible needs to be studied carefully. For example, the book *United in Worship of the Only True God* has this to say:

> Have you personally read the *entire* Bible? If not, make a spe-cial effort to do so. . . . Gaining *accurate* knowledge requires that we read carefully, and if a portion is deep we may need to read it more than once in order to grasp the sense of it. . . . To be sure, reading the Bible is a challenge—a project that we can beneficially work at for a lifetime.[4]

The Original Languages of the Bible

It must be understood that the Bible is the inspired word of God in the original language texts of the Bible as they have been preserved through manuscript copies. This means that no English translation is an absolutely perfect version of Scripture, though many if not most English versions are close enough to the original that the essential teachings of Scripture can still be found there. On this point the Jehovah's Witnesses fully agree. "No translation of these sacred writings into another language, except by the original writers, is inspired."[5]

Evangelicals and Jehovah's Witnesses also agree that the inspired text of the Old Testament (which they call the Hebrew Scriptures) is the Hebrew text, not the Greek or Latin transla-tions.[6] They also agree that the New Testament (which they call the Christian Greek Scriptures) inspired text is the Greek text, not Aramaic or Hebrew.[7] (Even though the Jehovah's Witnesses think, as do a few evangelicals, that Matthew may have been written originally in Hebrew or Aramaic, they apparently agree that the inspired version of Matthew is the Greek one which has been preserved.[8])

Finally, both agree that the text of the Bible that is considered God's word must be based on the original-language manuscripts that have survived throughout the centuries, especially the earliest and most complete. The Jehovah's Witnesses have indicated their belief in this principle by their following (generally) of the Masoretic text of the Hebrew Old Testament and the Westcott-Hort text of the Greek New Testament,[9] and by their insistence that God has preserved his word faithfully through the process of copying and recopying.[10] That the Jehovah's Witnesses recognize that God has preserved an accurate text is very important, since to deny this fact would be in effect to reject God's word.

The Verbal Accuracy of the Bible

It must be agreed that, although God allowed the individual styles of the biblical writers to be manifested in their writings, he nevertheless made certain that the words they used were perfectly suited to communicating the truths he wished written (2 Peter 1:20–21). Since God cannot lie (Titus 1:2), his word cannot deceive; therefore, the words of Scripture must be considered a reliable expression of the word of God. Correct interpretation of the Bible must assume that the writers used the right words, in the right grammatical form, in the right syntax (word order). Interpretations that overlook, ignore, or misconstrue the wording of the text are to be rejected. The Jehovah's Witnesses implicitly acknowledge this principle by their frequent appeal to vocabulary, grammar, and word order in defense of their interpretations of the Bible.[11]

The Totality of the Bible

Keeping 2 Timothy 3:16 in mind, we agree in rejecting what some theologians call a "canon within the canon," the notion that there are certain parts of Scripture that are more authoritative or more faithful to God's truth than other parts. For example, we reject the claim that the Old Testament has a less noble view of God than the New Testament. The Jehovah's Witnesses testify to their rejection of such a false view of the Testaments by their refusal to call them the Old and New Testaments.[12] Many evangelicals have pointed out the possible misunderstandings that might arise from these names, although nearly all evangelicals continue to use the names because they are in some sense accurate (the Old Testament does focus on the history of God's people under the old covenant, while the New Testament does introduce the new covenant).

To deny that one part of the Bible is more inspired or less inspired than another part does not indicate failure to recognize legitimate distinctions between various parts of the Bible. The Jehovah's Witnesses agree with this, as can be seen from their teaching that the Old Testament Law of Moses, including the Ten Commandments, is not binding on Christians.[13] While many (not all) evangelicals understand the Christian's relation to the Law differently from the Jehovah's Witnesses, the point is that at the least everyone involved agrees there are such distinctions within the Bible so that some parts apply today more directly than other parts, even though every part of the Bible is God's word and has something important for us to understand.

Reason and Truth

The Goal of Truth

Worship acceptable to God must be based on truth. *Truth* is here understood to mean reality, that understanding which corresponds with the way things actually are. This is how Jehovah's Witnesses also understand truth.[14] Although no human being's perception of truth will be exhaustive, perfect, or inerrant, it is still possible to know the truth in those basic issues of life that affect one's relationships with God and with other human beings.

The Normative Validity of Logic

It is here assumed that all honest persons will agree to abide by the principles of reason specified by the rules of logic. The sad truth, revealed in the Bible in such passages as Romans 3:4, 10–13, is that none of us is completely honest; therefore, we will all need God's mercy and favor if we are truly to think reasonably about the things revealed in the Bible. However, genuine Christians are those whose lives as a whole are committed to the truth, while non-Christians are those whose lives as a whole are based on falsehood and lies. Thus, non-Christians and those professing a false Christianity cannot help but be illogical and irrational when it comes to the big questions of life, unless by God's grace they repent. Christians, on the other hand, can be logical and rational to the extent that they have matured spiritually, morally, and intellectually.

To be reasonable means to think in a way that is not deceiving, that does not lead to falsehood. Although many people today reject logic and embrace the absurd or irrational, this book assumes that those involved in this dialogue will agree to put truth above feelings or personal convenience and therefore follow reason. Certainly the Jehovah's Witnesses agree on this point. Their handbook of questions and answers on various doctrinal topics is entitled *Reasoning from the Scriptures.* Thus, all I am attempting to do in this section is to spell out some of the implications of this principle.

The general point here is that it is inconsistent to claim to believe the Bible and yet fail to believe what logically follows from what the Bible says. For instance, it would be illogical to confess belief in the Bible's teaching that God has always existed, and then affirm that God had a beginning. It would be unreasonable to say with the Bible that stealing is wrong, and then insist that embezzlement is not wrong (even though the word *embezzlement* never appears in the Bible). Such inconsistent affirmations would show that one either did not understand or simply rejected what the Bible was really saying.

On the other hand, we must be very careful not to apply principles of reason improperly or in a way that actually contradicts the Bible itself. The Jehovah's Witnesses believe that they avoid such misuse of reason, as can be seen from the following statement from *Reasoning from the Scriptures*: "So they [Jehovah's Witnesses] do not resort to philosophical arguments to evade its clear statements of truth or to justify the way of life of people who have abandoned its moral standards."[15]

For instance, the reasoning that says if God were loving he would never punish people but always unconditionally accept them is improper for two reasons: First, the conclusion (God would never punish people) does not follow necessarily from the premise (God is loving), because such a line of reasoning actually assumes a certain understanding of "loving." That is, some people reason as follows: Being loving *means* accepting people no matter what and never punishing them; God is loving; therefore, God will never punish people. But in fact the Bible makes it clear that God's love is a holy, righteous love that *includes* righteous punishment of unrepentant sinners. Second, the Bible actually states both that God is loving and that he does punish people; therefore, any reading of the Bible that is correct must somehow embrace both teachings, even if some people have a very hard time putting the two ideas together.

That the Watchtower officially teaches that faulty or illogical reasoning should be avoided was recently confirmed in an article in *Awake!* entitled, "Five Common Fallacies—Don't Be Fooled by Them!" The article correctly defines *fallacy* as "a misleading or unsound argument, one in which the conclusion does not follow from preceding statements, or premises."[16] It then discusses in some detail five common fallacies, giving examples. The article concludes, "So don't fall for fallacies."[17] I will be making further references to this important article as we go along.

Rejection of "Ad Hominem" Arguments

An *ad hominem* (Latin, "against the man") argument attempts to discount a position by attacking the person who holds it rather than the person's reasons for holding it. One kind of *ad hominem* argument assumes that everything believed by certain groups or individuals is false. This assumption, if consistently followed, leads to falsehood. Thus, someone may argue that:

   (a) Atheists believe that there is no God.
   (b) Everything atheists believe is false.
   (c) Therefore, there is a God.

Believers in God can all agree that (a) and (c) are true statements and may therefore suppose that (b) is also true. However, that such is not so can be seen from this:

   (m) Atheists believe that the world is real.
   (n) Everything atheists believe is false.
   (o) Therefore, the world is not real.

Another kind of *ad hominem* argument is what the *Awake!* article previously cited calls "attacking the person," a fallacy which involves "making an irrelevant attack on the person" presenting an argument. The article rightly points out that attacking a person's character or intelligence is no substitute for answering his or her arguments.[18]

It follows from the above that truth-seeking people should agree not to reject the other side's arguments simply because they regard those others as unbelievers. Rather, they should respond only to the arguments. While people are entitled to regard those who believe in doctrines different from theirs as "apostate" or "cultic," they are not entitled to dismiss their beliefs on that basis. That is, the only way to know that a group is apostate is if its teachings are false; it is therefore circular reasoning (see below) to argue that a group's teachings are false because they are apostate. Dialogue is impossible where one or both sides are convinced that the other side has nothing worthwhile or valuable or true to say.

In some sense the Jehovah's Witnesses agree that the reasonable person is one who is willing to listen to and consider another person's point of view. For example, *Reasoning from the Scriptures* makes the following statement about its purpose, a statement I can apply to my own book:

> This publication has not been prepared for the purpose of helping anyone to "win arguments" with people who show no respect for the truth. Rather, it provides valuable information that is meant to be used in reasoning with individuals who will allow you to do so. Some of them may ask questions to which they really want satisfying answers. Others, in the course of conversation, may simply state their own beliefs and they may do so with some conviction. But are they reasonable persons who are willing to listen to another viewpoint? If so, you can share with them what the Bible says, doing so with the conviction that it will find welcome response in the hearts of lovers of truth.[19]

Truth as Noncontradictory

All reasonable persons must agree that truth never contradicts truth. The Jehovah's Witnesses agree fully with this principle as it applies to the Bible. For example, *Reasoning from the Scriptures* advises Jehovah's Witnesses to respond to claims that "the Bible contradicts itself" by saying that they have never seen an actual contradiction in the Bible and then asking for a specific example.[20]

Although this principle is completely valid, it must be applied carefully with full regard for the nature of language. Two statements that appear contradictory may not be if one or more key terms are used differently in the two statements. For example:

(a) It is raining.
(b) It is not raining.

These two statements are not necessarily contradictory. Perhaps (a) was spoken on Tuesday and (b) on Wednesday; or (a) in Seattle and (b) in Dallas. Or perhaps in (a) *raining* means precipitation of any kind, while in (b) *raining* means fairly heavy precipitation (as opposed to drizzling, for example). An oversimplistic or overliteral approach to language will result in seeing contradictions where there are none.

Avoidance of Circular Reasoning

Also called begging the question, circular reasoning is the fallacy of "proving" one's point by assuming its truth. Usually this assumption is unstated and implicit rather than explicit. In the following discussion Tom's argument is circular:

> Tom: Reagan couldn't have lied about Iran-contra.
>
> Tim: What makes you so sure?
>
> Tom: Because Reagan is an honest man.

So is Joe's argument in this exchange:

> Joe: The Bible is the word of God.
>
> Jim: How do you know that?
>
> Joe: It says so in the Bible.

The truthfulness of the conclusion does not make the argument itself valid. Regarding the second argument, there are better ways to show the truth of the Bible based on its own testimony, but the above simplistic argument is circular in a way that is completely unpersuasive. Any productive discussion must avoid such circular reasoning.

Avoidance of All Fallacious Arguments

There are many other common errors of reasoning that all honest people will wish to avoid in the course of any discussion. We cannot explain and illustrate them all here, but in general, we may say that any argument that if applied in the same form to another issue would lead to what both sides would rightly recognize as falsehood must be either fallacious or based on one or more false premises (assumptions). The following are examples of such fallacies.

Equivocation is a word used in two different senses in an argument that treats those two senses as identical. Here is a silly example: "Henry is a king; a king is a playing card; therefore, Henry is a playing card."

Hasty generalization is a sweeping generalization based on less than sufficient examples. Here is an example: "The last three kings have been named Henry; therefore, all kings are named Henry."

Argument from silence is an important fallacy because it is so often used. It occurs when people argue that because something is not mentioned by someone, that person does not think it is true (or, they think it does not exist). Here is an example: "Mary did not call Henry a king; therefore, Mary does not think that Henry is a king." In general we may say that silence proves nothing unless we have a clear warrant for expecting something to be said. For example, the Bible claims to contain all the information we need to know to be saved (2 Tim. 3:15–17). Therefore, if someone were to say that we must wear white robes to be saved, we would rightly dismiss such a claim by pointing out that the Bible says nothing of the kind.

Argument from (fallible) authority reasons that a person's word is proof enough of something simply because he or she is more knowledgeable on the subject than most others (although that person is fallible). For example: "Dr. Janet Jones, who is a historian, says Henry was not a king; therefore, Henry was not a king." Dr. Jones may be right, but we are entitled to ask *on what basis* she makes this statement.

The *Awake!* article quoted earlier cites this fallacy as a "form of verbal intimidation" and devotes more attention to this fallacy than to any of the other four it discusses. In this connection it should be noted that the article claims that "clergymen today are known to resort to similar tactics when unable to prove from the Bible such teachings as the Trinity, the immortality of the soul, and hellfire."[21] I certainly agree that "clergymen" have sometimes reasoned in this fallacious way and make no defense for such reasoning. However, it seems fair to ask Jehovah's Witnesses to consider whether they have ever made illegitimate appeals to fallible authorities to support their views. It is easy to "throw stones" at others for their fallacious reasoning; what is harder is to admit that we ourselves have at times been guilty as well. I raise the question here only to encourage Jehovah's Witnesses to resolve not only to avoid being fooled by others' use of fallacies, but also to avoid using fallacies as well.

In conclusion, I urge evangelicals and Jehovah's Witnesses alike to study logic. In recent years evangelicals have begun producing some helpful treatments of logic from a Christian perspective.[22] More important than learning rules about logical reasoning, however, is maintaining a firm commitment to honesty, integrity, accuracy, and truth. No one will ever be eternally lost because they failed to master logic, but many, many will be lost for accepting false doctrine on the basis of what they should have known was faulty reasoning.

Interpreting the Bible's Truth

The principles of biblical interpretation discussed in this section should be obviously true, once one has accepted the principles discussed so far in this chapter. Again, in theory the Jehovah's Witnesses should have no difficulty recognizing these as valid.

Don't Depend on One Translation

No one English translation is to be regarded as the only reliable version. Differences of translation are to be resolved *only* by exegesis (close interpretation) of the text in question, not by appeals to fallible authority, as we just saw. Thus, the fact that one or more scholarly translations adopt a particular rendering does not of itself validate or justify that rendering. We want to know what the text *really* says, not what some scholars say it says or what it *might* say. I will address the specific question of the New World Translation in chapter 4; but it should be noted that the Watchtower Society makes frequent reference to other translations as well and has even published editions of the King James Version and the American Standard Version of 1901. So in principle this guideline should meet no objection.

Use Scholarly Reference Works as Tools

The same holds for the use of scholarly reference works such as lexicons, grammars, commentaries, dictionaries, word studies, encyclopedias, histories, theological works, etc. All have their place and may help us to ascertain what the Bible means, but none of them is infallible or exhaustive. Where facts or sound reasoning show that such works are right, they are right; where such show them to be wrong, they are wrong. None of us should argue that a particular text may be interpreted to have a certain meaning merely because some scholars say so.

On the other hand, if all or nearly all biblical scholars agree on something, and they advance good reasons for their position, and no sound reason can be given for rejecting it, their position may be regarded as established. Scholars are servants of those of us who are seeking truth.

Consider the Whole Teaching of Scripture

Anything and everything the Bible says that is relevant to a particular question should be considered in formulating doctrine, so as to avoid hasty generalizations. That doctrine which most accurately incorporates all of the relevant biblical data must be considered the Bible's teaching.

Treat Explicit Statements as Foundational

In seeking to answer a particular question, explicit statements in Scripture should be treated as foundational and primary. For example, suppose we are trying to determine whether God is a man (as in Mormon beliefs) or a spirit. John 4:24 says explicitly that God is spirit, and passages such as Numbers 23:19 say explicitly that God is not a man. These passages should govern our study, and passages that talk about

God's "eyes" or "hand" should be understood figuratively in light of the explicit statements above. (Such figures of speech are *anthropomorphisms*, meaning that they speak of God as if he were a man, even though he is not.) Note that this is a little different from saying that "unclear" or "ambiguous" passages should be interpreted in light of "clear" passages. People often say passages are "unclear" when they seem to contradict their own theology and "clear" when they seem to confirm their beliefs. This is simply a subtle form of circular reasoning (which has already been shown to be fallacious).

Give Context Due Consideration

This is a principle of interpretation which almost everybody professes to know and few follow. Certainly Jehovah's Witnesses recognize that biblical passages should be interpreted in keeping with the context.[23] By *context* is meant the historical situation in which the text was written, the kind of writing of which the text is a part (poem, historical narrative, letter, etc.), and the surrounding words and statements of which the text forms a unit.

In taking context into account, it is important to avoid the abuse of "overcontextualizing." This is often done in two ways. One way is to limit general statements or universal principles to the specific situation in which they are applied. For example, simply because Paul's command to "pursue righteousness, faith, love, peace" (2 Tim. 2:22a) was given directly to Timothy in the context of a warning to flee youthful lusts (2:22b) does not mean that only young people should pursue these things! Another way to overcontextualize is to seize some aspect of the general context and ignore the specific context to justify a particular interpretation. For example, certain groups argue that only the Book of Acts contains the apostles' gospel of Christian salvation, because the Gospels present Jesus before the Christian church existed, while the epistles are written to people who are already Christians. This plausible-sounding argument ignores the fact that both the Gospels and the epistles make specific references to the gospel and to salvation.

Avoid Relating Unrelated Texts

It is a common error to bring together two or more un-related texts of Scripture and thereby derive a doctrine or prac-tice completely foreign to the Bible. The humorous example of the man who brought together "Judas went out and hanged himself" and "Go thou and do likewise" is well known. A more serious example is the Mormon argument that Jeremiah 1:5 compared with John 8:56–58 proves the preexistence of all human beings as spirit children of God. Presumably Jehovah's Witnesses would have no trouble recognizing the validity of this principle.

Don't Depend on Etymology to Reveal Meaning

The word *butterfly* looks like *butter + fly*, but this does not tell us much about the meaning of the word. The word *good-bye* etymologically was a contraction of *God be with you*, but not everyone who says "good-bye" believes in God. The Greek word *ekklesia* ("church," "congregation," "assembly") derives from *ek + kaleō*, but does not mean "called-out ones," as is sometimes popularly asserted. The word *ekballō* does mean "cast out," but obviously can be used without implying the idea of physically throwing something. Etymology can be helpful, but it is not definitive for determining the meaning of words.[24] As far as I know this point is not discussed in Jehovah's Witness publications, but it is not something they should have trouble seeing as valid.

Give Each Passage of Scripture Its Full Weight

This principle balances the above principle to treat explicit statements as foundational. It is improper to force Scripture passages to fit your doctrinal beliefs by "shoehorning" them into your system. A common way of doing this is to appeal to supposedly clear texts to muffle troublesome texts. For exam-ple, Oneness Pentecostals (who teach that Jesus is God the

Father) deny the plain meaning of passages such as John 8:16–18 (where Jesus says that he and the Father are two persons) by appealing to Isaiah 9:6 (where in most translations Jesus is called "everlasting Father"). This is just as wrong as denying or twisting the truth of Isaiah 9:6 to make it fit John 8:16–18. The proper approach is to interpret both passages fairly by careful attention to the words and the context, and then compare what they *really* say. I assume that this principle would also be agreeable to Jehovah's Witnesses, although I am not aware of any explicit reference to it in their writings.

Interpret Narratives in Light of Teaching Passages

Narrative passages do have teaching purposes, but their meaning must be determined by God's "commentary" on the events as found in the didactic portions of Scripture. In reporting the polygamy of believers before the time of Christ, for example, the Bible does not say that they sinned; but from various didactic passages we know what God's will is in this matter. On the other hand, didactic texts cannot be used to deny the explicit statements of narrative texts. Again, I see no reason why Jehovah's Witnesses should not agree to this principle.

Don't Confuse Literal and Figurative Meanings

Again, everyone recognizes this principle in theory, including Jehovah's Witnesses, but few people have thought through how to apply it properly. (In making this observation, I do not claim that I have arrived at a perfect or infallible ability to distinguish the two myself.) The temptation sometimes is to define *figurative* as "what I don't want to believe literally." Rather, we should take the Bible literally except where the context itself indicates the word or statement should be taken figuratively. It can do this, for example, by the kind of writing it is (a poem, song, or apocalyptic prophecy is more likely to use symbolic or figurative language than a history or letter). Spiritual realities (such as the nature of God, the effects of God's work in human lives) are likely to be described in figurative language. Once again, a key aspect to success in Bible study is considering everything the Bible has to say on a particular subject. The Jehovah's Witnesses have pointed out the importance of interpreting biblical symbolism on the basis of other passages in the Bible rather than on speculations not based on the Bible itself.[25]

Believe the Bible Even When You Don't Understand It

This follows from the simple fact that God's knowledge is admittedly far greater than ours. We simply must face the fact that some things about God are revealed in the Bible to be true even though we as human beings cannot fully comprehend them. God doesn't reveal nonsense, but he does reveal things which to finite, sinful humans may *seem* like nonsense. If a human father can ask his child to trust him when he tells him things he can't understand, how much more should we be willing to believe whatever God has revealed in his word, even if we can't understand it. The Jehovah's Witnesses do admit that at least in some sense the Bible does teach things that are beyond human comprehension.[26] However, they do not take this nearly as far as do evangelicals. I shall have more to say about this issue in chapter 5.

Recognize the Fact of Progressive Revelation

We are speaking here about progressive revelation within the pages of the Bible, not about any kind of progressive revelation since the close of the canon of Scripture. (There may be progressive understanding of the Bible on the part of God's people, but this progressive understanding is not the same as the progressive infallible revelation in Scripture.) There are some things that God simply did not reveal right away, because his people were not ready to hear them (see John 16:12; Eph. 3:5).

Later truth never contradicts earlier truth, but it may supplement it or complete it; and later commands may replace earlier ones. An example of progressive revelation is the gradual manner in which God revealed truth about the coming

Messiah to Israel in the Old Testament. It is apparent that Abraham knew less about the Savior than Isaiah did; and even more apparent that neither of them knew nearly as much as did John the Baptist; and that John the Baptist knew less than did Peter and Paul. Each of them undoubtedly had misconceptions about the Savior, though these misconceptions did not form a part of their inspired teaching. What they knew, they knew, and they were saved by believing what God had told them. Again, I assume that in principle Jehovah's Witnesses will agree, although the way in which they work it out in practice will differ from the way evangelicals do.

Seek the Interpretation Which Best Fits the Text, Not the One Which Best Fits Your Doctrines

This is a rather general principle to which all of us should give assent. The Jehovah's Witnesses' affirmation that they do not seek to avoid the Bible's clear statements[27] shows that they agree. Whether or not someone adheres to this principle can be tested by noting whether he or she consistently considers all of the relevant aspects of the text as well as other interpretations besides his or her own. When people quickly jump to a conclusion about a text without considering important questions about their own interpretation, they likely are simply seizing upon an interpretation because it fits their preconceived beliefs.

With the foregoing principles in mind concerning the truth of the Bible, the exercise of reason, and the interpretation of the Bible, dialogues about the Bible between people who disagree on its teachings are more likely to result in constructive progress toward truth. Those who by God's grace honestly seek to understand God's word must keep these principles in mind if they are to be certain of reaching their goal.

2

Evangelicals,
Jehovah's Witnesses,
and the Bible

Why do evangelical Christians and Jehovah's Witnesses
derive such vastly different beliefs from the Bible? We
shall begin by considering how both evangelicals and
Jehovah's Witnesses have typically answered this question.

Same Problems, Different Perspectives

Evangelicals have generally made the following comple-
mentary observations about what divides them from Jehovah's
Witnesses:

1. Jehovah's Witnesses do not have the Holy Spirit illu-
   minating them to accept the truth of what the Bible

39

really says and therefore distort it according to their sinful preconceptions.

2. Jehovah's Witnesses do not employ proper methods of interpretation in their reading of the Bible and thus are prone to arrive at erroneous conclusions as to its teaching.

3. The real authority for Jehovah's Witnesses, regardless of their claim to base everything on Scripture, is actually the Governing Body, a group of leaders who rule the entire movement and dictate to their followers what they will believe through the publications of the Watchtower Bible and Tract Society.

4. The Bible used by Jehovah's Witnesses, the New World Translation (NWT), is doctrinally biased and thus cannot be considered a reliable version of the Bible.

All of these observations are relevant up to a point, even from a Jehovah's Witness perspective. Thus the Jehovah's Witnesses would give more or less the same kind of answers, as follows:

1. Evangelicals and other non-Witnesses lack the guidance of "holy spirit" because of their rejection of God's channel of spiritual guidance, God's organization.

2. Evangelicals and other non-Witnesses employ faulty methods of interpretation.

3. Evangelicals and other non-Witnesses are bound to err in their reading of the Bible because of their failure to accept the instruction of God's organization. Indeed, to reject the organization is to reject the Bible, since the Bible indicates that the organization is God's servant through which he instructs his people.

4. The NWT is the only unbiased modern translation of the Bible. All other versions of the Bible are unduly influenced by doctrines and practices which Christendom as a whole has adapted from paganism.

Evangelicals and Jehovah's Witnesses strongly disagree on where the fault lies, but they would appear to agree that these factors—attitudes toward the Watchtower organization, differing translations, the Holy Spirit (or "holy spirit"), and interpretive methods—are what separate true from false interpretations of the Bible.

In this book, I shall argue that evangelicals are basically right in their perspective on these problem areas. However, in my view these considerations, though relevant, do not tell the whole story. I shall argue that we must look beyond these factors for a more basic, foundational explanation of the disparity between the Jehovah's Witnesses' and the evangelicals' interpretations of the Bible. Such an explanation will also need to account for these four distinct factors as well.

Two of the factors—the authority of the Jehovah's Witness organization and the use of the New World Translation—are so important that I will devote separate chapters to them. In the remainder of this chapter I will discuss the other two factors—the Holy Spirit and principles or rules of biblical interpretation.

Who Has the Spirit?

It is certainly true that persons who claim to believe the Bible but who are not illumined by God's Spirit will develop a distorted understanding of Scripture. Thus evangelicals and Jehovah's Witnesses can agree that whoever is guilty of holding such distorted interpretations does so, on one level at least, because they do not have God's Spirit (whether they believe in the "Holy Spirit" as a divine person, as evangelicals do, or "holy spirit" as an impersonal force directed by God, as do Jehovah's Witnesses[1]).

There are, however, two limitations in this observation. The first is that it applies universally to all human beings except true Christians. All non-Christians distort and deny biblical teachings until God's Spirit enlightens them to see the truth of what the Bible says.

Thus, from an evangelical standpoint, the Jehovah's Witnesses' lack of the Holy Spirit is a significant factor in their denying biblical truth, but it does not at all explain why Jehovah's Witnesses take their particular line of interpretation. (For example, it does not help to explain why Jehovah's Witnesses interpret the Bible as they do rather than as do members of The Way International or the Worldwide Church of God, two other sects which claim to believe the Bible as infallible truth.) That is, the factor is essentially negative: It tells us why non-Christians do not believe the Bible or why they hold distorted interpretations of the Bible, but it does not help us understand why various non-Christians hold differing attitudes toward the Bible and come away with markedly different readings of its teachings.

The same would have to be said, from a different perspective of course, from a Jehovah's Witness standpoint. The alleged lack of "holy spirit" might be said to account negatively for evangelicals' rejection of Jehovah's Witness doctrines, but it could not explain positively why evangelicals hold the particular views they do.

The other limitation is that this factor is not something that can be openly, publicly identified with some groups rather than others. That is, who is being guided by God's Spirit and who is not can only be determined on the basis of previously determined beliefs about who or what God's Spirit is and what doctrines and practices are validated by God's Spirit. From an evangelical standpoint, even though evangelicals may confidently say that Jehovah's Witnesses do not have the Holy Spirit, pointing this out to the Jehovah's Witnesses is useless because they think they do have God's Spirit and that evangelicals do not. What is at issue is not the necessity of illumination by God's Spirit, but how that illumination takes place and what that illumination will lead someone so illumined to understand the Scriptures to teach.

Rules for Reading the Bible

Another factor which evangelicals and Jehovah's Witnesses often regard as accounting for their divergent interpretations of the Bible is whether or not proper procedures are used in reading the Bible. Evangelicals in particular have consistently criticized Jehovah's Witnesses for violating such basic rules of interpretation as considering the immediate context of a verse or taking statements in their normal sense wherever possible. Similarly, Jehovah's Witnesses argue that non-Witnesses who profess faith in the Bible do not take biblical statements in context and do not consider everything the Bible says on certain doctrinal matters.

This factor, more than the other three discussed at the beginning of this chapter, is directly hermeneutical in nature, especially as it relates to what I have called prescriptive hermeneutics (the study of how one ought to interpret the Bible). As an evangelical, I do maintain that Jehovah's Witnesses regularly abuse such principles of interpretation when they seek to demonstrate that their unbiblical views are biblical. Any interpretation of the Bible that is heretical is going to be in conflict with the precise wording and the literary and historical contexts of the statements being misinterpreted (recall our discussion of these points in the first chapter). It is one thing to claim that another's interpretation is in such conflict with the text, and another thing to show it. Later in this book, in the final two chapters, I shall discuss specific examples of the way Jehovah's Witnesses interpret the Bible.

Nevertheless, it would be overly simplistic for an evangelical to say that failure to follow such principles or rules of interpretation explains *why* Jehovah's Witnesses interpret the Bible as they do. I say this for the following reasons.

First, many of these rules of interpretation are stated explicitly in Watchtower publications, as was documented in chapter 1. Evangelicals such as I contend that in practice Jehovah's Witnesses often do not follow these principles, but the problem does not appear to be simple ignorance.

Second, when Jehovah's Witnesses defend beliefs which coincide with those of evangelicals, they appear to observe these interpretive principles. This is especially evident in their books and articles on family life and personal morality (although there are some differences here with evangelicals which I do not want to be misunderstood as denying). I would expect Jehovah's Witnesses to make similar concessions about evangelical uses of the Bible, particularly since Watchtower publications often cite evangelical works when these agree with their beliefs (and sometimes even when they do not!).[2]

Third, saying that someone's misinterpretation of the Bible is caused by mere ignorance of rules of interpretation implies that their misunderstanding of Scripture is morally excusable. In one sense those who distort the Bible are ignorant, but their ignorance is of a morally culpable sort. Thus the apostle Peter warns that the "untaught [or ignorant] and unsteady are twisting [the Scriptures] . . . to their own destruction" (2 Peter 3:16 NWT). I do think it is true that Jehovah's Witnesses misunderstand as well as misapply even those sound principles of interpretation which they do recognize. However, underlying this failure to employ accurately sound principles of interpretation must be some more foundational *spiritual* failure, as 2 Peter 3:16 surely implies. I shall have something to say about this aspect of the problem in a later chapter.

Finally, their use of unsound methods of interpretation seems more a reason for Jehovah's Witnesses' continuing in their beliefs than for their initial adoption of them. While some Jehovah's Witnesses may have embraced their beliefs only after making a thorough study of the entire Bible through the use of the Witnesses' interpretive methods, this is probably the exception rather than the rule. Typically people embrace a religious position as a totality because they are persuaded of the truth of certain key aspects of it, and only after accepting the system do they begin a long (often lifetime) process of studying the other religious beliefs directly. This is as true of evangelicals as it is of anyone else, and it is not a bad thing. People cannot be expected to postpone making a religious commitment until after they have mastered all of the doctrinal complexities associated with their religious system and all of the relevant biblical material. Indeed, the Bible is quite clear that God calls us to commit our lives to him and then as committed believers to learn all that he has to teach us. Jesus Christ calls us to become disciples (learners) and *as such* to grow in our understanding of his will.

What can and should be expected is that as individuals progress in their study of the Bible they will abandon unbiblical notions and embrace the biblical system in progressively greater faithfulness. Moreover, since the purpose of the Bible is primarily to bring people into a saving relationship with God, and only secondarily to instruct them in a system of doctrine, it may be expected that persons who read the Bible with the illumination of God's Spirit will come immediately to a basically sound understanding of who God is and of what he requires of those whom he saves (even though this understanding will need to be further refined).

These two standard areas of concern between evangelicals and Jehovah's Witnesses—the illumination of God's Spirit and methods of interpretation—are both significant in explaining why Jehovah's Witnesses continue in their beliefs. Neither of them, however, is a positive factor in explaining why Jehovah's Witnesses adopt the particular beliefs that they do. I shall explore this question directly in a later chapter. However, in the next two chapters I shall discuss the Jehovah's Witnesses' organization and the New World Translation, as these are generally considered to be most influential in determining Jehovah's Witnesses' beliefs.

3

The Watchtower: *Biblical Servant or Unbiblical Master?*

It is universally argued by evangelical critics of the Jehovah's Witnesses that their beliefs are based on the authoritative teachings of their religious leaders in the Watchtower Bible and Tract Society. In one sense this is quite true. Certainly the Jehovah's Witnesses today learn their doctrine from the Society's publications and representatives, a fact the Witnesses themselves generally would not dispute. And the publications of the Society are filled with warnings to follow the organization's teachings without question.[1]

For example, the 1952 *Watchtower* taught that whatever is put before the Witness as "spiritual food" is to be "eaten" without question:

We should eat and digest and assimilate what is set before us, without shying away from parts of the food because it may not suit the fancy of our mental taste.[2]

47

Nearly thirty years later the same point was made:

> If we have once established what instrument God is using as
> his "slave" to dispense spiritual food to his people, surely
> Jehovah is not pleased if we receive that food as if it might
> contain something harmful. We should have confidence in the
> channel God is using.[3]

According to Jehovah's Witnesses, the Bible cannot be
understood apart from the *Watchtower* magazine and other
Watchtower publications. This is illustrated by such testimonies as the following:

> A special pioneer making a return visit asked the lady what
> book teaches us the will of God. "*The Watchtower*, of course,"
> she said. Our sister proceeded to explain that it was, rather,
> the Bible. "Yes, but what would I do with my recently obtained
> Bible if I did not use *The Watchtower* to understand it?"[4]

Jehovah's Witnesses are therefore expected to study carefully
and believe everything that the *Watchtower* magazine says:

> It is all-important to study the Bible and, since *The Watch-
> tower* assists in understanding the Bible, its study is also
> imperative. . . . If we have love for Jehovah and for the organi-
> zation of his people we shall not be suspicious, but shall, as
> the Bible says, "believe all things," all the things that *The
> Watchtower* brings out. . . .[5]

The result is that the Witnesses regard the Watchtower
publications, especially the *Watchtower* magazine, as coming
from God, and thus as virtually inspired, even if in theory
they admit the publications are not inspired or infallible.
The following testimony, reported in the *Watchtower* itself, is
typical:

> The brother went down to get the mail before breakfast, and
> when we had breakfast he said, "Brother Reimer, I got a new
> *Watchtower* this morning, and do you know the first thing that
> Ma and I do when we get that *Tower?* We kneel down before we

take the wrapper off and ask Jehovah to make us worthy to see
what the message is that Jehovah has for us."[6]

Although the Watchtower Society publications are thus
accorded an authority that is beyond questioning, in my opinion evangelicals have overstated the significance of the
Watchtower Society's authority for the Jehovah's Witnesses'
belief structure. Some important qualifications need to be
made if the importance of this factor is not to be exaggerated
and the evangelicals' proper criticism thereby dismissed by
Jehovah's Witnesses.

Is the Watchtower an Extrabiblical Source of Authority?

By the Watchtower Society I do not mean merely one of the
legal corporations bearing that name. In this sense there are
actually many Watchtower Societies. Rather, when I speak of
the Watchtower Society I have in mind the leaders of the
Jehovah's Witness "organization" who control the Watch Tower
Bible and Tract Society of New York (located in Brooklyn) and
the Watchtower Bible and Tract Society of Pennsylvania.
Together these two corporations control the teachings and
practices of Jehovah's Witnesses worldwide. The Brooklyn
corporation, known as Bethel, functions as the international
headquarters of the Jehovah's Witness religion. The leaders of
the Brooklyn corporation, who are responsible for the contents of the religious publications it produces, are known col-
lectively as the Governing Body, and are regarded by Jehovah's
Witnesses as having a special authority from God.

Some Jehovah's Witnesses, in private conversations and discussions with evangelicals, have found it useful to deny that
God's organization is to be identified with the Watchtower
Society. The Watchtower Society, they argue, is actually only a
corporation that God's people use to get their work done. This
technicality does not, however, alter the facts. The leaders of
the Watchtower Society in Brooklyn are not merely administer-
ing a corporation, they are controlling the doctrines believed

by the millions of Jehovah's Witnesses worldwide. In earlier Watchtower publications, and later especially in publications meant for Jehovah's Witnesses only, references to the Society as God's organization are common. Note, for example, the following statement which appeared in the 1919 *Watchtower:*

> Is not the Watch Tower Bible and Tract Society the one and only channel which the Lord has used in dispensing his truth continually since the beginning of the harvest period?[7]

Another example comes in the 1943 *Informant,* a publication for Witnesses only:

> Today all the faithful ones work together in unanimity under the direction of Christ Jesus. His instructions are sent out through the Theocratic organization which the Lord has brought forth in the earth, "the Society." It is composed of the "proved faithful brethren," having been tried by the Lord and gained this approval. Therefore you should have perfect confidence in the tried and proved faithful Society and stick closely to it for your own good.[8]

It should be noted that the term *the Society* in Watchtower literature can refer narrowly to the corporation or corporations through which the leaders direct and govern the religion worldwide, or it can refer broadly to what the Witnesses call the "anointed" class, the class of Christians through whom God channels his teaching. For example, the 1923 *Watchtower* stated: "The word *Society* as used herein is a generic term applied to the body of consecrated, anointed Christians throughout the world. . . ."[9]

The 1983 book *United in Worship of the Only True God* makes it clear that God's organization is the publisher of Watchtower literature:

> To help us to use and understand the Bible, Jehovah's organization supplies excellent Scriptural material in *The Watchtower* and related publications.[10]

The 1981 *Watchtower* asserted about its own publishers:

> At the Brooklyn headquarters from which the Bible publica-
> tions of Jehovah's Witnesses emanate there are more mature
> Christian elders, both of the "remnant" and of the "other
> sheep," than anywhere else on earth.[11]

If they do say so themselves! In one sense, therefore, evangelicals are quite right to say that the Jehovah's Witnesses
regard their organizational leaders as an authority alongside
the Bible. However, the Watchtower Society and its publications are not regarded by Jehovah's Witnesses as an infallible source of truth alongside the Bible. The Society's own
publications disavow any claim to prophetic inspiration or
infallibility, and admit that erroneous interpretations of
Scripture and mistaken predictions supposedly based on
Scripture have been made by them in the past.

For example, the *Watchtower* made the following dis-
claimer: "However, *The Watchtower* does not claim to be
inspired in its utterances, nor is it dogmatic."[12] In 1981 the
Watchtower admitted:

> True, the brothers preparing these publications are not infalli-
> ble. Their writings are not inspired as those of Paul and the
> other Bible writers. (2 Tim. 3:16) And so, at times, it has been
> necessary, as understanding became clearer, to correct views.
> (Prov. 4:18)[13]

The 1985 book *Reasoning from the Scriptures* actually admitted that Jehovah's Witnesses have held mistaken views, but
justified their mistakes by claiming that the apostles also held
wrong views: "Jehovah's Witnesses do not claim to be inspired
prophets. They have made mistakes. Like the apostles of Jesus
Christ, they have at times had some wrong expectations."[14]

The Jehovah's Witnesses' view of the authority of the Watchtower Society and its publications, then, is complex, and from
the outside appears to involve some inner tensions. Though
not claiming actual infallibility, the Society's warnings to the
Witnesses not to question any of the organization's teachings

amounts to a *pragmatic* equivalent to infallibility. "The organization's publications make mistakes, but assume that everything they say is correct until the organization itself says otherwise," is the message. Jehovah's Witnesses frequently argue that the proper course is to accept humbly whatever their leaders teach, even if it seems obviously wrong, trusting that if they are wrong God himself will correct them in his due time.

> Jehovah and Christ direct and correct the slave as needed, not we as individuals. If we do not see a point at first we should keep trying to grasp it, rather than opposing it and rejecting it and presumptuously taking the position that we are more likely to be right than the discreet slave. We should meekly go along with the Lord's theocratic organization and wait for further clarification. . . .[15]

Moreover, although the Witnesses deny that they regard their publications as inspired, at least until quite recently the Society's publications have likened the organization's allegedly accurate predictions to those of biblical prophets. For instance, in a 1972 article the *Watchtower* magazine cited the Society's prediction before the fact of the demise of the League of Nations as evidence that the Jehovah's Witnesses constitute a corporate "prophet."[16] Their *1983 Yearbook*, speaking of those Witnesses who will be among the 144,000 and who are thus considered spiritual leaders in the organization, refers to this class as "the 'prophet' whom Jehovah has raised up" today.[17]

More recently their inaccurate predictions have been excused on the basis that biblical prophets and apostles made similarly inaccurate predictions and had imperfect understanding of what God had revealed to them.[18] This implies that they have not really stopped thinking of their leadership as comparable to the prophets and apostles of the Bible. Yet they deny that the leaders' writings have the infallibility of Scripture. This amounts to the leaders claiming the authority of the biblical prophets and apostles (whatever they teach publicly or write is to be accepted as truth) without the responsibility to be as truthful as those inspired men were.

Although it is true that biblical prophets made mistakes, they did not make such mistakes when they were prophesying. No genuine biblical example of an error in prediction or doctrine can be found in the prophetic teaching of any true prophet of God in the Bible. The alleged instances of such "mistakes" do not hold water.

Consider some of the alleged "mistakes" by biblical prophets and apostles cited by Witnesses.[19] Daniel 12:9 and 1 Peter 1:10–11 prove only that the prophets did not always understand fully the meaning of their own prophecies—not that some of what they actually prophesied was in error. First Corinthians 13:9–10 means that prophecy gives us only partial knowledge of the future and will be done away when the future itself becomes reality. Though such knowledge is partial, it is all true; it is not partly true and partly false. Proverbs 4:18 is about the way the righteous live (their "path"), not about progressive prophetic revelations (and even if it were, it would not imply error in the early stages, merely less information). Luke 19:11, John 21:22–23, and Acts 1:6–7 talk about the false notions held by the apostles and other disciples, but none of these texts say that the apostles taught these false notions as part of the prophetic word of truth. Nathan's first word to David concerning building a temple to "do all that is in your heart" (1 Chron. 17:2) was not claimed by Nathan to be a word from God, whereas his subsequent message that David was not to build the temple is specifically said to be a word from God (17:3–15). This last point is so obvious that it seems the Jehovah's Witness responsible for this example either did not read carefully or deliberately misused the text.

Another commonly cited example of a biblical prophet supposedly making a "mistake" is Jonah's prophecy of judgment on Nineveh. Since Jonah prophesied, "Yet forty days and Nineveh will be overthrown" (Jonah 3:4), and Nineveh was not overthrown in forty days, Witnesses claim that Jonah made a mistake yet, of course, was not a false prophet.

This argument, however, is seriously flawed. First of all, it is clear from the text of Jonah that Jonah himself did not make a mistake. Jonah said exactly what God told him to say. The Jehovah's Witnesses, on the other hand, do not claim that they published exactly what God wanted said concerning the various dates they had set for the end of "this system of things." Supposedly they admit to having erred themselves due to their own imperfections. If that is so, the example of Jonah, an inspired prophet who spoke exactly the words God gave him to say, is irrelevant to their case.

Moreover, it is evident that Jonah's prophecy was not in error, because it was implicitly conditional. The Ninevites understood Jonah to mean that their city would be overthrown in forty days *unless they repented* (Jonah 3:5–9). God understood Jonah's prophecy, which was, after all, God's own message, in the same way (Jonah 3:1, 10). Even Jonah understood that the message he delivered was intended to be a means of extending God's grace and mercy to the Ninevites (Jonah 4:1–2). Thus, all of the parties involved—God, the Ninevites, and Jonah—understood the prophecy to be conditional.

The same cannot be said for the erroneous predictions the Jehovah's Witnesses have made concerning Armageddon. Neither the Jehovah's Witnesses nor the non-Witnesses to whom they have been preaching have ever understood the dates they have given for the end—1914, 1918, 1925, and 1975—to be conditional.

The Jehovah's Witnesses' attempts to equate their leaders with biblical prophets in terms of authority while disavowing infallibility should not be taken to imply that the Witnesses think the Bible itself contains errors, or that they think of their leaders as equal in authority to the Bible. It is simply an inconsistency in their thought which they do not perceive as such. Jehovah's Witnesses do not have an obviously extra-biblical source of authority comparable to that, say, of the Mormons, who regard three other works besides the Bible as "scripture" (the Book of Mormon, Doctrine and Covenants, and Pearl of Great Price). Nor do they attribute error to the Bible in the way that Mormons and other modern sects do.

On the other hand, the Jehovah's Witnesses do have authoritative leaders whose teachings are regarded as *virtually* infallible, as not to be questioned, and as having an exclusive authority from God. In this regard the Jehovah's Witnesses are similar, for example, to such modern sects as The Way International and the Worldwide Church of God. Thus the question whether Jehovah's Witnesses have an extrabiblical authority cannot be answered in a black-or-white way. By their own theory they do not, but in practice they do treat the Watchtower as a functional extrabiblical authority.

The Circularity of Watchtower Authority

The Society's authority works to reinforce the Jehovah's Witnesses in their beliefs but rarely, if ever, to initiate them into those beliefs. That is, people do not accept Jehovah's Witness beliefs because they first accept the organization's authority, but rather the reverse—they embrace Witness beliefs and on that basis accept the organization as authoritative.

Indeed, one important criticism that may justly be leveled against the Watchtower publications concerns their repeated insistence that the Bible is unintelligible to those who do not accept the Society's authority. In order to prove that no one can understand the Bible apart from God's organization on earth, the Jehovah's Witnesses appeal to a battery of texts from the Bible which supposedly say or imply that such is true. Unfortunately, such an argument implicitly contradicts the very thing it is supposed to prove. If no one can understand the Bible apart from submitting to the teaching of the organization, then no one can understand these specific texts apart from the organization. But if that is so, then no one can know that these passages teach the necessity of submitting to the organization's teaching unless they are already submitted to it!

This problem will be encountered no matter how many verses the Jehovah's Witnesses quote in seeming support of their claim. Passages from the Bible simply cannot prove to those outside one's camp that only those who follow the camp leaders can understand the Bible. If someone who was outside the camp and not already in submission to the camp leaders was able to read and understand such passages, it would disprove at once the camp leaders' claim that the Bible is a closed book to those who do not submit to their teaching.

Put another way, the argument is both self-contradictory and circular (recall our commitment in chapter 1 to avoid both kinds of fallacious reasoning). It is circular as follows: (1) God's organization says you need it to understand the Bible because (2) the Bible itself says so, and you know the Bible says so because (3) God's organization says so. It is self-contradictory because the appeal, "Read these verses in the Bible and you will see that you need God's organization to understand the Bible" implies *both* "You can understand the Bible" and "You cannot understand the Bible."

One way to escape this circle is to say that at least some of the Bible can be understood apart from God's organization—those passages which teach the necessity of God's organization, and perhaps others—while others cannot be understood apart from the organization. The problem with such a claim, if it were to be made (and to my knowledge the Witnesses have never put forward such a claim), is that there is nothing in the Bible to indicate that some of its statements are understandable to the masses and others are understandable only to the "initiates." Such a claim, in fact, would contradict the Bible's teaching that *all* human doctrines are to be tested by God's word (Acts 17:11; Gal. 1:8).

Another alternative for the Witnesses would be to admit frankly that, in their view, no one outside of their camp can understand these passages until they submit to their organization. The implication of such an admission, however, would be that they would no longer have any basis for quoting Scripture at all to back up their teachings when talking to non-Witnesses. Their entire witnessing effort, to be consistent, would have to consist of urging outsiders to accept the organization to gain access to understanding any of the Bible.

A third approach the Jehovah's Witnesses might take to this dilemma would be to say that the Bible is understandable apart from the organization, but it is the organization's responsibility to guide God's people in their understanding of the Bible, and anyone who understands and accepts the Bible's teaching will in fact submit to the organization. This, however, would be a different claim altogether, and one which the Witnesses cannot afford to make. In general, people who do not accept without question everything the organization says tend not to continue believing the Witnesses' doctrines once they have become thoroughly familiar with the Bible. Even Jehovah's Witnesses who have been rigorously schooled in their organization's teachings and who have served faithfully for years tend to lose faith in those teachings once they begin to study the Bible at all independently. By "independently" I mean not in a spirit of prideful disdain and disregard for everything the organization publishes, but simply reading the Bible itself without constantly referring to Watchtower publications for the authoritative interpretation of each verse.

The Jehovah's Witnesses have admitted that Bible study apart from Watchtower publications does indeed lead people away from Jehovah's Witness doctrine. In an often-quoted statement from an article in the September 15, 1910, issue of the *Watch Tower,* the founder of the Jehovah's Witnesses, Charles Taze Russell, maintained that:

> Furthermore, not only do we find that people cannot see the Divine Plan in studying the Bible by itself, but we see, also, that if anyone lays the SCRIPTURE STUDIES aside, even after he has used them, after he has become familiar with them, after he has read them for ten years—if he then lays them aside and ignores them and goes to the Bible alone, though he has understood his Bible for ten years, our experience shows that within two years he goes into darkness. On the other hand, if he had merely read the SCRIPTURE STUDIES with their references, and had not read a page of the Bible, as such, he would be in the light at the end of two years, because he would have the light of the Scriptures.[20]

A little over seventy years later, the *Watchtower* issued a similar warning:

> From time to time, there have arisen among the ranks of Jehovah's people those who, like the original Satan, have adopted an independent, faultfinding attitude. . . . They say that it is sufficient to read the Bible exclusively, either alone or in small groups at home. But, strangely, through such "Bible reading," they have reverted right back to the apostate doctrines that commentaries by Christendom's clergy were teaching 100 years ago. . . .[21]

What, then, about those Bible passages which the Witnesses claim say we must follow the organization's teaching? It is one thing to say that such a claim does not make sense; it is another thing to show that in fact the Bible says no such thing. We need, then, to look at the proof texts used by the Witnesses in defense of their claims to unique authority in interpreting the Bible.

"The Faithful and Discreet Slave"

The major text on which Jehovah's Witnesses base their claim that accurate biblical teaching can be found only in their organization is Matthew 24:45–47, where Jesus gives the following parable (all biblical citations in the rest of this chapter are from the New World Translation [NWT]):

> "Who really is the faithful and discreet slave whom his master appointed over his domestics, to give them their food at the proper time? Happy is that slave if his master on arriving finds him doing so. Truly I say to YOU, He will appoint him over all his belongings."

The Jehovah's Witnesses' argument, in a nutshell, is that this passage teaches that no one can understand the Bible apart from this faithful and discreet slave, interpreted to mean Christ's anointed followers viewed as a group, with the Governing Body acting as the administrative part of the slave through its control of the teachings and practices of the Jehovah's Witnesses.[22] A number of difficulties with this interpretation of Matthew 24:45–47 may be mentioned here. Jesus' parable does not end with verse 47, but goes on in verses 48–51 to issue this warning:

> "But if ever that evil slave should say in his heart, 'My master is delaying,' and should start to beat his fellow slaves and should eat and drink with the confirmed drunkards, the master of that slave will come on a day that he does not expect. . . ."

The usual Jehovah's Witness interpretation of this second part of the parable is that the evil slave is Christendom, that is, all professing Christian religions and denominations apart from the Witnesses. However, Jesus' expression "that evil slave" suggests that he is speaking generally of two types of people who profess to serve him, those who are faithful and those who are evil. The point of the parable, then, would be that Christian leaders must be faithful in their service; if they are, when Christ returns, they will be given even greater responsibility, and if they are disloyal, they will be punished.

Such is explicitly the point of the same parable in the parallel passage in Luke 12:41–48. After commending the faithful servant by saying, "Happy is *that slave*" and promising that the master "will appoint him over all his belongings," Jesus continues:

> "But if ever *that slave* should say in his heart, 'My master delays coming,' and should start to beat the menservants and the maidservants, and to eat and drink and get drunk, the master of *that slave* will come on a day that he is not expecting. . . ."

Thus, comparing the two versions of the same parable makes it clear that Jesus is not speaking of the faithful and discreet slave as a single organization or group permanently distinguished from the evil slave. Rather, Jesus is speaking generically of a slave, someone supposedly serving Christ, and says that the same slave has the potential either to serve him well and be rewarded or serve him ill and be punished. Jesus' whole point is that it is possible for men appointed to the task of feeding God's people to be unfaithful to the point of being evil, regardless of what organization they are a part.

Moreover, the exhortation of this parable is directed toward those who consider themselves to be Christ's slave, not to those who are "fed" by the slave. Nothing in this parable suggests, as the Society implies, that the domestics are supposed to eat whatever (if anything) the slave puts before them, no matter what it is. At the end of the parable, the rewards and punishments spoken of are meted out to the slaves for their faithfulness or lack of it, not to the domestics for their cooperation in eating everything the slaves fed them. Thus, the parable is not a warning to believers to accept uncritically everything some teacher or group of teachers tells them God's word says.

Yet another problem is that in the Witnesses' understanding of the parable a fundamental inconsistency or incoherence appears through their explanation of the parable. As has already been noted, the Witnesses identify the "faithful and discreet slave" as the anointed Christians as a group. Thus the slave has been described as "the collective body of the anointed remnant," or "the entire Christian congregation made up of the 144,000 disciples who have been begotten by God's spirit," or "a remnant of those spiritual 'brothers' of the reigning King Jesus Christ."[23]

However, in the parable the slave dispenses food at the right time to the domestics. And here comes the problem: according to the Witnesses, the domestics are the anointed Christians also! This forces the Witnesses to argue that while the slave represents the anointed as a *group*, the domestics represent the anointed as *individuals*. The 1988 reference work *Insight on the Scriptures* explains: "Thus the entire anointed Christian congregation was to serve in a united stewardship, dispensing such truths. At the same time the individual members making up such composite body, or the 'domestics' making up the 'house' of God (Mt 24:45; Heb 3:6; Eph 2:19), would also be *recipients* of the 'food' dispensed."[24]

The problem here is that if the individuals who make up the slave and the domestics can be the same, then there is no reason to maintain that the slave is a group distinct from other Christians at all—distinct, say, from a group represented by "all his possessions" (Matt. 24:47), which the Witnesses say represent the "great crowd."

One other problem of a different sort may be mentioned. The Witnesses argue that no one can understand God's word correctly without submitting to the teaching of the faithful and discreet slave. Yet, in their view, there was no such slave for almost nineteen centuries. This is quite easy to prove. In the Witnesses' view, the slave is an earthly *organization* that speaks for Jehovah—not merely scattered individuals or home study groups, but a single organization responsible for the spread of the gospel throughout the earth. As has already been noted, the anointed Christians as individuals are represented in Jesus' parable, according to the Witnesses, by the domestics, not by the slave. This means that the slave can only exist as a collective, organized group of the anointed acting together.

Now, if such an organization had existed in the late nineteenth century, there would have been no need at all for C. T. Russell and his associates to separate from Christendom and begin a "modern work." As soon as the Bible Students (as Jehovah's Witnesses were originally known) discovered the earthly organization, they would simply have allied themselves with it. Since, instead, they created a new organization, it follows that there was no faithful and discreet slave on earth for centuries. The implication is that God had no true representatives on earth and did not intend for people to understand the Bible until Russell and his friends came along—a conclusion which is very hard to justify biblically (see Matt. 16:18; 28:20; Eph. 4:11–16; Jude 3).

Other "Organization" Proof Texts

We can briefly examine several other proof texts the Jehovah's Witnesses cite to defend their ascribing sole interpretive authority over the Bible to the Watchtower Society. In Acts 8:30–31 Philip asks the Ethiopian eunuch if he understands what he is reading (Isa. 53:7–8), to which the eunuch replies, "Really, how could I ever do so, unless someone guided me?" Certainly this passage does indicate the need of *guidance*, or help, in studying the Bible, but it does not prove that some organization exists whose pronouncements on biblical interpretation may not be challenged. In this passage we find one Christian preaching Christ directly from the Bible, not an organization with a magazine or a book, and an individual who is baptized on his confession of faith and is sent on his way rejoicing—with no organization he must join. While it is true that Philip was not working as a lone individual accountable to no one and in cooperation with no one, neither was he working as a mere mouthpiece of an organization.

The Witnesses often cite 2 Peter 1:20–21, with emphasis on its disavowal of "private interpretation," as a refutation of the "Protestant principle" that every Christian is responsible for reading and obeying the word of God. However, Peter here is not talking about Christians interpreting the Bible, but about how the Bible came to be written originally. As one Watchtower reference work has correctly explained, "Thus, the Bible prophecies were never the product of astute deductions and predictions by men based on their personal analysis of human events or trends."[25]

If we read on in 2 Peter, the very next words of the apostle are a warning concerning false teachers (2:1) who lead people astray into certain judgment (2:2–22). The way to avoid "destructive sects" (2:1), according to Peter, is to "remember the sayings previously spoken by the holy prophets and the commandment of the Lord and Savior through YOUR apostles" (3:2). That is, the way to tell true teaching from false teaching is to compare the teaching with what the Bible itself says, not, as the Jehovah's Witnesses argue, by appeal to what God's organization says the Bible means.

Proceeding to the end of Peter's letter, the apostle warns his readers against "the untaught and unsteady" who twist the Scriptures "to their own destruction" (3:15–16). The Society's publications have cited this Scripture also to validate their authority. However, the false teachers in this text are in error because they are "untaught and unsteady," that is, they have not been thoroughly grounded enough in the Scriptures as students first, and are spiritually immature and unstable. Their error is *not* due to lack of conformity with some organization.

Indeed, had Peter been a Jehovah's Witness, no doubt he would have gone on to say something like, "Knowing this, remain faithful to the teachings of God's organization." Instead, he writes:

> YOU, therefore, beloved ones, having this advance knowledge, be on YOUR guard that YOU may not be led away with them . . . but go on growing in the undeserved kindness and knowledge of our Lord and Savior Jesus Christ (3:17–18).

Another text regularly cited in this connection is Acts 15, where the apostles and elders in Jerusalem are called upon to give a ruling on the question of whether Gentiles had to convert to Judaism before being accepted as Christians (Acts 15:1–35). This account is considered by Jehovah's Witnesses to be a model example of the first-century "governing body" in action. This argument cannot stand in the light of the fact that Jehovah's Witnesses do not claim that their "governing body" has apostles in it. Once again the tension between the Jehovah's Witnesses' attributing apostolic authority but not apostolic status to their leaders leads them into serious mishandling of Scripture.

Finally, the Witnesses also cite the words of Peter to Jesus, "Whom shall we go away to?" (John 6:68) and apply them as follows: Where shall we go for instruction in the Bible if we leave the Watchtower? This interpretation of John 6:68 is seen, for example, in the following statement in the 1981 *Watchtower:*

> Rather, the record that the "faithful and discreet slave" organization has made for the past more than 100 years forces us to the conclusion that Peter expressed when Jesus asked if his apostles also wanted to leave him, namely, "Whom shall we go

away to?" (John 6:66–69) No question about it. We all need help to understand the Bible, and we cannot find the Scriptural guidance we need outside the "faithful and discreet slave" organization.[26]

Peter's next words, though, suggest something different. "You have sayings of everlasting life; and we have believed and come to know that you are the Holy One of God" (6:68–69). In fact, the Witnesses have left out the first word of the sentence they do quote: "*Lord,* whom shall we go away to?" Surely the problem here does not need much spelling out. To apply to a human organization these words which acknowledge Jesus as Lord and the only hope of eternal life is both foolish and blasphemous.

The authority the Watchtower leadership claims does not have a biblical basis, and involves the Witnesses in considerable tension with the Bible's teaching on Christian leaders. The Bible indicates that even the teachings of apostles and prophets are to be tested by Scripture (Acts 17:11; 1 Thess. 5:20–21). The Jehovah's Witnesses' unwillingness to put their own leaders' teaching to this test is therefore a disobedient stance that prevents them from understanding the Bible correctly.

On the other hand, we repeat that neither belief nor nonbelief in the Watchtower organization accounts for why some people accept Jehovah's Witness beliefs in the first place and others do not. At most, their acceptance of the organization accounts for Jehovah's Witnesses continuing in their beliefs even when they become aware of tensions between those beliefs and the teachings of Scripture.

4

The New World Translation

The New World Translation (NWT) has been enormously instrumental in helping Jehovah's Witnesses to feel continued confidence that their beliefs are biblical. The whole work, but especially the New Testament portion (what Jehovah's Witnesses call the Christian Greek Scriptures), is carefully designed to import Witness beliefs into the text and screen out, as much as a seemingly literal translation can, the traditional Christian beliefs rejected by Jehovah's Witnesses. As I shall try to illustrate in this chapter, the NWT is filled with faulty translations designed to make the Bible fit Jehovah's Witness doctrine. It is therefore legitimate to say, as evangelicals consistently maintain, that the NWT is doctrinally biased.

In this chapter I do not intend to present a thorough demonstration of the doctrinal biases of the NWT. Instead I shall try to give several brief examples of the kinds of mistranslations I regard as evidence of a pervasive doctrinal bias in the

NWT (restricting the examples to the Christian Greek Scriptures). In most cases the reader can verify what is said quite simply by consulting the Witnesses' own *Kingdom Interlinear Translation of the Greek Scriptures*. The *KIT* prints the 1984 edition of the New Testament portion of the NWT on the right side of the page. On the left side is the Westcott-Hort Greek text of 1881 with the Society's own 1969 word-for-word interlinear translation printed beneath the Greek words. The editors of the *KIT* explain the purpose of the work: "The word-for-word interlinear translation and the *New World Translation* are arranged in parallel on the page, so that comparisons can be made between the two readings. Thus, the accuracy of any modern translation can be determined."[1]

There are several types of mistranslations in the NWT. In this chapter I can do no more than draw attention to some of the most common and unfortunate.

Adding *Other*

As has often been noticed, in Colossians 1:16–20 the word *other* is added four times in the NWT to make it appear that Christ is part of creation. Paul is thus made to say that "all [other] things" were created in and for Christ, as if Christ were one of the created things. The addition of the word *other* is usually justified by an appeal to such texts as Luke 11:41–42 and Luke 13:2, 4, where the word *other* is also added after the word *all*. However, in these passages (and in others where the same practice is rightly followed) the addition of *other* does not change the meaning, but simply makes for smoother English. In Colossians 1:16–20, however, whether one adds *other* makes a great deal of difference to the meaning.

What is not so often noticed is that the NWT does this same thing in several other passages as well (Acts 10:36; Rom. 8:32; Phil. 2:9). In Romans 8:32, the word *other* is not even placed in brackets, contrary to the work's stated practice. In all of these texts, the intent seems to be to undermine the implication of the text that Jesus Christ is God.

Other Additions

There are several other texts where the NWT adds words which change the text's meaning without placing them in brackets. Some of these have real doctrinal significance. In Romans 8:28 *all things* is changed to *all his works*. This implies that God does not work *all* things together for good to those that love God, but only those things which he himself does, over which he has control.

In Philippians 1:23–24 several words are added without brackets that, along with some other changes, completely alter the structure and thereby also the meaning of the text. The passage reads in the NWT (with the added words italicized): "I am under pressure from *these* two things; *but what* I do desire is the releasing and the being with Christ, for this, *to be sure*, is far better." There are other errors as well, but the additions indicated here clearly change the meaning so as to avoid the text's implication that at death Paul would be with Christ.

Some of the additions in brackets in the NWT so clearly change the meaning it is a wonder that more Jehovah's Witnesses do not question them. In 1 Corinthians 14:12–16 the phrase *gift of the* is added in brackets five times, changing "spirit" to "[gift of the] spirit." The result is that Paul's contrast between his own personal "spirit" and his "mind" is removed. To assure that this contrast is missed, the word *my* is also added in brackets before *mind* twice in verse 15 but not before *spirit*. Thus the simple contrast between "the spirit" and "the mind" (or "my spirit" and "my mind," NASB) is changed to "the [gift of the] spirit" and "[my] mind."

Words Omitted

The NWT occasionally omits key words when to include them may contradict Jehovah's Witness doctrine. The most glaring example is Romans 8:1: "Therefore those in union with Christ Jesus have no condemnation," which omits the word *now*. This omission is evidently motivated by the fact that the Witnesses do not believe anyone can claim *now* to be free of condemnation.

Also notable is Colossians 1:19: "because [God] saw good for all fullness to dwell in him." Here the little word *the* is omitted before *fullness*. This is significant, because in the NWT rendering "all fullness" is ambiguous, whereas "all *the* fullness" clearly refers to the fullness of God's own being (compare Col. 2:9).

John 14:14 should also be mentioned. In the NWT this reads: "If YOU ask anything in my name, I will do it." The Greek text in the KIT, however, has *me* after *ask*, so that it should be translated: "If you ask *me* anything in my name, I will do it." It is true that some later Greek manuscripts omitted this word, but most of the earlier ones included it, and most modern editions of the Greek New Testament include it. At the very least, the NWT ought to have mentioned this reading in a note.

Translating *In*

It is possible to make too much of prepositions. Such words as *in*, *of*, *into*, and *with* really do not in and of themselves have any doctrinal significance. It is only as these words are used in relation to other words that they take on meaning. It is also important to respect the fact that a preposition has different meanings in different contexts. Having said all that, prepositions do have recognizable functions and meanings and cannot be translated in whatever manner one chooses. In this regard the NWT translates the simple preposition *in* (Greek, *en*) with an unnecessary variety and in some places translates it in ways that obscure or alter the meaning of the passage.

It is not simply that the word *en* is usually translated "in union with" when Christ is the object of the preposition. "In union with Christ" instead of "in Christ" is paraphrase, not translation, but it is not necessarily a bad paraphrase. What is objectionable is when *en* occurs several times in a short passage and is translated two or three different ways, not to make the meaning clearer but to obscure the real meaning.

For instance, in 1 John 5:20 the NWT reads in part: "And we are in union with the true one, by means of his Son Jesus Christ." Reading this translation, one would never suspect that "in union with" and "by means of" translate the same simple Greek preposition. Nor is there any sound reason for this variation. "And we are in union with the true one, in union with his Son Jesus Christ," would have brought out John's point that union with Christ *is* union with God.

Again, in Colossians 2:6–12 "in him" and "in whom" (*en autō, en hō*) becomes "in union with him" (v. 6), "in him" (vv. 7, 9), "by means of him" (v. 10), and "by relationship with him" (vv. 11, 12). These variations serve no useful purpose, undermine the unity of the passage, and obscure the point of the passage, which is that the Christian life consists solely of a supernatural relationship with Christ through faith.

There are many other passages where *in* is paraphrased to avoid the otherwise clear meaning of the text. For example, in Matthew 5:19 *in* becomes "in relation to" so as to avoid the passage's teaching that some who disobey the Law's commandments and teach others to do so will nevertheless be accepted "in the kingdom of heaven" (which Jehovah's Witnesses believe will be restricted to 144,000 specially chosen and sanctified believers).

Only Believe?

One of the most offensive teachings of evangelical Christianity to the Jehovah's Witnesses (and to many others as well) is that God reckons the sinner righteous through simple faith, or believing, in Christ. Of course, where faith or belief is reduced to mental assent to a doctrine, such a view of faith is rightly rejected. But the biblical teaching is that such free justification is based on faith in *Christ*, not faith in a doctrine. Even this teaching is offensive to the Jehovah's Witnesses, as can be seen in the attempt to obscure this truth in the NWT.

Most notable in this regard is the rendering of "exercise faith" instead of "believe." As others have noted, to exercise faith implies more than to believe; it implies doing works on the basis of one's belief. The NWT almost always translates the Greek word for "believe" (*pisteuō*) as "exercise faith" when it concerns God's free pardon and justification of those who believe in Christ (John 1:12; 3:16–18 [but note v. 15]; Rom. 4:3; Gal. 3:22). It is true that genuine faith results in good works motivated by love (James 2:14–26; Gal. 5:6; 1 Tim. 1:5; 1 John 3:14–18), but the condition laid down in Scripture for God's declaring the sinner righteous before him is faith alone, not works. Good works are the fruit, not the root, of salvation.

No *Spirit*

It was already noted that in 1 Corinthians 14:12–16 the phrase *gift of the* is added in brackets five times, changing "spirit" to "[gift of the] spirit." The NWT elsewhere frequently paraphrases the simple word *spirit*, especially when referring to the immaterial aspect of human nature, to avoid the implication that such a spirit has a reality distinct from the body. For instance, in Hebrews 12:19 "the Father of spirits" (or, "the spirits") becomes "the Father of our spiritual life." In Galatians 6:18 "your spirit" is paraphrased "the spirit YOU show."

Similar rewordings are introduced in passages where the simple translation "spirit" or "Spirit" might imply that God's Spirit is a person, contrary to the Jehovah's Witnesses' doctrine that "holy spirit" is God's "active force." So, Jude's description of certain men as "not having the Spirit" (or, more literally, "not having spirit") is rendered "not having spirituality" (Jude 19).

Even clearer is 1 John 4:1–6. John has just stated that we know our union with God is secure "owing to the spirit which he gave us" (3:24). The next sentence in the NWT reads: "Beloved ones, believe not every inspired expression, but test the inspired expressions to see whether they originate with God" (4:1). One would never suspect from this rendering that "inspired expression" translates the same Greek word (*pneuma*) as "spirit" in 3:24 (see also 4:2, 3, 6). John's whole point is that although the Spirit's presence assures us of God's love, we are not to believe every "spirit" that claims to be from God but test each one by the teachings its prophet espouses, "because many false prophets have gone out into the world" (4:1). The NWT obscures this point to avoid the implication that God's Spirit is a person rather than a force (just as the demonic spirits are personal entities and not impersonal forces, as the Witnesses recognize).

The same doctrinal bias can be seen in 1 Timothy 4:1, where the NWT reads: "However, the inspired utterance says. . . ." A straightforward "the spirit says" would too obviously imply the personality of the "spirit."

Words for God

Finally, the way in which the NWT most systematically distorts the teaching of the Scripture is in its handling of the names (or, names and titles) of God. Two points must be made here.

First and most obvious to anyone who has looked at the NWT is the appearance of *Jehovah* in the New Testament portion over two hundred times where the Greek text has *kurios* ("Lord"). I will discuss this matter in detail in chapter 8.

The second way in which the NWT has systematically abused the divine names or titles is in its handling of texts in which Jesus is called God. In nine Bible texts Jesus is definitely called God (Isa. 9:6; John 1:1, 18; 20:28; Rom. 9:5; Titus 2:13; Heb. 1:8; 2 Peter 1:1; 1 John 5:20; possibly also Acts 20:28). Of these, the NWT translates four so that Jesus is not called God at all (Rom. 9:5; Titus 2:13; Heb. 1:8; 2 Peter 1:1), and two so that he is "a god" or "god" (John 1:1, 18). The remaining three texts (Isa. 9:6; John 20:28; 1 John 5:20) are not mistranslated, but are interpreted so that either Jesus is not called God at all or he is called God only in some lesser sense. In short, wherever possible, the NWT translates texts that call

Jesus God in such a way as to keep the text from making that identification.[2]

The Case for Bias

Only a small sampling of mistranslations in the NWT have been documented here. We have seen words added, words omitted, and words and phrases paraphrased improperly in the service of shoehorning the Bible into Jehovah's Witness doctrine. We have seen such mistranslations conveniently supporting the distinctive Watchtower denials of several Christian doctrines: the deity of Christ, the personhood of the Holy Spirit, the separableness of the human spirit from the body, spiritual life after the death of the body for Christians, God's absolute sovereign control over the world, the unity of God's people, and justification by faith. Were we to extend the study we would see that every distinctive doctrine of the Jehovah's Witnesses has somehow been insinuated into the text of the NWT in a way that to the non-Witness clearly shows doctrinal bias.

One possible criticism of this survey may be that it does not anticipate the arguments Jehovah's Witnesses would advance in defense of their controversial renderings in the NWT. In response I would say, first, that it is my experience, and doubtless that of most others, that no Jehovah's Witness will admit there may be so much as *one* doctrinally slanted verse in the NWT. But to defend such a position they must satisfactorily explain *all* of the examples given here (and many more that could be given). Second, the deeper treatment a specific text is given, the more evidence piles up that the NWT renderings are wrong and biased, as I have sought to illustrate in a previous book on John 1:1 and John 8:58.[3]

In chapter 7 of this study, a specific passage of the Bible will be examined as a case in point. I shall argue that the methods and presuppositions of biblical interpretation used by the Jehovah's Witnesses are seriously flawed and lead them inevitably into error. Since this case study involves a text that is mistranslated in the NWT, it will serve to reinforce the point made here that the NWT systematically distorts the Bible to fit the teachings of the Watchtower.

But Is It Scholarly?

In this chapter I have presented briefly a substantial body of evidence from the pages of the NWT itself to support a charge of religious bias. However, this does not of itself prove that the NWT is *unscholarly*. Brilliant scholars conceivably might use their considerable intellectual resources to produce a translation of the Bible which fits their preconceived doctrinal beliefs. Nor would this prove that they were necessarily conscious of their bias; advanced scholarship in a narrow field such as translation does not make a person any more aware of his prejudices and biases than is the less educated layperson.

Thus the question, so often debated, of whether or not the translators of the NWT were scholars, or whether the NWT should be regarded as a scholarly work, is not terribly relevant to the question of the reliability of the NWT. The alleged endorsements of the NWT by scholars, often cited by Jehovah's Witnesses in defense of the NWT, cannot prove its accuracy in the face of the evidence already examined. In fact, most of these supposedly scholarly endorsements are of questionable origin or of questionable value as support for the NWT (see Appendix A on this point). But this is more interesting for what it tells us about the honesty of those compiling these endorsements than what it tells us about the NWT itself.

The fact is that the NWT shows evidence that those responsible for the revisions, the marginal notes, and the appendices, while not bona fide biblical scholars, are quite capable of handling scholarly reference works and using them to develop their own interpretations of the Bible. This is much more true of the 1984 reference edition than it was of the original 1950 edition of the *New World Translation of the Christian Greek Scriptures*, but that only shows all the more that increased scholarship does not bring with it increased accuracy in the face of strong biases.

It would therefore be a mistake for evangelicals to rest their case against the NWT solely or primarily on the amateur status of its translators. The principal member of the original translation committee, Fred Franz, was indeed an amateur translator—he had not completed college, had not produced any publications in scholarly journals or through scholarly publishing houses—and that shows in many ways. But the case against the NWT must rest on the evidence from within the NWT itself; and this, as we have seen, is sufficient to warrant the conclusion that the NWT is an unreliable translation of the Bible.

Putting the New World Translation in Perspective

As important as the NWT is for controlling Jehovah's Witnesses' understanding of the Bible, the use of the NWT cannot explain why most Jehovah's Witnesses embrace Watchtower doctrines initially. Most people who become Jehovah's Witnesses convert to it after some nominal Christian experience, usually including possession of a Bible. The Jehovah's Witnesses frequently cite other Bible translations in defending their views. Moreover, the New Testament portion of the NWT did not appear until 1950. Thus, for over half a century people accepted Jehovah's Witness beliefs without the aid of the NWT.

I do not deny that the NWT may be helpful to the Jehovah's Witnesses in leading persons into their belief system, since it must prove useful to be able to point to a Bible that does reflect their doctrinal views. Yet it would not appear to be a principal factor, for the reasons given.

5

The Foundation
of Jehovah's
Witness Beliefs

What foundational assumption or preconception forms the real basis for Jehovah's Witnesses' understanding of the Bible? Although there are different ways of approaching this question, I shall begin with a historical perspective. What led the first "Jehovah's Witness," Charles Taze Russell, to interpret the Bible as he did? (The Jehovah's Witnesses, of course, did not go by that designation until after Russell's death; in his day they were known as Bible Students.) Although on some points of doctrine the contemporary Witnesses differ with Russell, on all of the major doctrinal issues separating them from evangelicals their views are basically the same as those of Russell and the first Bible Students. After examining the hermeneutical foundation of Russell's own beliefs, I shall turn to current Watchtower publications to

show that this same presupposition is foundational for
Jehovah's Witnesses today.

Russell and Reason

Charles Taze Russell[1] was born in 1852 in Pittsburgh,
Pennsylvania. His father, Joseph L. Russell, raised Charles
first in the Presbyterian church and later in the Congre-
gational church. Russell was taught from the Westminster
Catechism and probably also the Westminster Confession of
Faith (the standard Calvinist confession for Presbyterians
and Congregationalists).

Thus Russell's first religious teaching was of a Calvinist sort.
There were different varieties of Calvinism in late nineteenth-
century Pennsylvania, and I do not know to which variety
Russell was exposed. However, from later patterns in C. T.
Russell's thinking it appears that he was familiar with a rationalistic strain of Calvinism that was particularly influential in nineteenth-century New England Congregationalism.
Judged from a more classically Calvinist or Reformed perspective, this system overemphasized logical consistency, pre-
destination, human inability to do God's will apart from grace,
and the eternal punishment of the wicked. By rationalistic I
mean an approach to truth that expects all beliefs to be comprehensible (that is, fully understandable in all its aspects) to
man's mind and that studiously avoids paradox and mystery
as far as possible. Such rationalism was nearly pervasive in
nineteenth-century America, and Russell evidently took such
rationalism for granted.

During his teen years Russell came to have doubts about
his Calvinistic beliefs. By the time he was sixteen he had
found "the logic of infidelity," that is, the arguments urged by
unbelievers against the Bible and Christian faith, so com-
pelling that he abandoned faith in the Bible at all "as soon as
I began to think for myself."[2] The biblical doctrine with which
he clearly had the greatest difficulty was that of eternal punishment, or "hellfire" as it was popularly called. Russell, as did

the "infidels," found this doctrine impossible to square with the doctrine of an all-loving God.

About a year later, Russell heard the preaching of an Advent Christian minister named Jonas Wendell. The Advent Christians, similar to the Seventh-day Adventists, were part of the larger Adventist movement, and like the Seventh-day Adventists denied eternal punishment in hell.[3] Russell credited Wendell's teaching with restoring his faith in the Bible. By 1870, when Russell was only eighteen years old, he had formed a Bible study group which was eventually to develop into what are now known as Jehovah's Witnesses.

Three somewhat related aspects of Adventist teaching appear to have been highly influential in reconciling Russell's rationalistic mindset with belief in the infallibility of the Bible. The first, already mentioned, was the Adventist denial of eternal punishment. Adventists argued that the Bible taught that *hell* in the Bible refers always to the grave, that the soul is not immortal but is annihilated when the body dies, and that the Bible does not teach eternal punishment. Russell took over this interpretation of the Bible's teaching on death and the soul virtually verbatim. To this day Seventh-day Adventist and Jehovah's Witness polemics against eternal punishment run remarkably parallel, often involving the same biblical proof texts and the same arguments relating to those proof texts. A small but apparently growing minority within evangelicalism today also appears to be adopting a similar viewpoint.

The second Adventist teaching that influenced Russell was the speculation concerning the fulfillment of biblical prophecies relating to Christ's second coming (or advent). Adventism was founded on the teaching of William Miller, a New York Baptist who had predicted Christ's return in 1843 and then 1844. After these predictions proved false, Miller, to his credit, abandoned Adventism, but some of his followers developed a rationale that kept the date of 1844 as a chronological marker of events that allegedly took place in heaven. At first Russell did not accept the Adventist chronological speculations, but they clearly stimulated in him a fascination with biblical prophecy and Christ's second coming. By 1876 he became convinced, largely through the teaching of Nelson H. Barbour (an Adventist who had been associated with Jonas Wendell), that Christ's advent was an invisible, spiritual presence, and that it could be shown from biblical chronology to have begun in 1874.

In fairness to Russell it should be observed that in his day fascination with relating biblical chronology to current events was widespread in England and America among evangelicals generally and not just Adventists. Although most evangelicals today denounce date-setting, some continue to engage in such speculation. Sometimes this speculation generates widespread interest among evangelicals, as in the recent stir over Edgar Whisenant's claim that the Bible indicated fall 1988 (he later said 1989) as the time of the "rapture," a sudden removal of Christians from the earth which Whisenant and many evangelicals think will occur seven years prior to Christ's return.[4] Many people initially become interested in the Bible and even come to believe in the Bible's inspiration because of such erroneous speculations.

The third Adventist teaching to have influenced Russell concerned the doctrine of God. Although most Adventists today are trinitarian and believe that Jesus Christ is the almighty God, a significant number of Adventists in the late 1800s did not. Many held to what is usually called an Arian view of Christ, that is, believing that Christ was a powerful angelic spirit created by God before he created anything else (a view similar to that held by the fourth-century followers of Arius, known as Arians). This view was apparently held by George Stetson, another Advent Christian minister whom Russell credited with influencing his doctrinal views. Thus it appears that the particular variety of Adventism which influenced Russell held to an Arian doctrine of Christ and rejected the Trinity. Russell first publicly identified himself with these views in 1882 after splitting with most of the other Adventist leaders who had associated with him.

The importance of these aspects of Adventist thought on Russell's thinking was that they enabled him to develop a system of doctrine in keeping with his rationalistic presuppositions. The doctrine of annihilation enabled him to avoid what he saw as a contradiction between God's love and God's sentencing people to eternal torment. The denial of the Trinity enabled him to avoid the apparent contradiction of three persons in one God. Thus these two aspects were for him important because they made God understandable. The fascinating study of biblical chronology and prophecy, involving an array of mathematical calculations, made the Bible seem scientifically credible in a day when Darwinism and historical criticism were widely regarded as undermining its credibility.

A good case can therefore be made that it was this rationalistic approach to religion that was foundational for Russell's own beliefs. His rationalistic desire to comprehend God and his truth led Russell first to abandon faith in the Bible, and then to accept it again on the condition that the Bible be interpreted in keeping with his reasoning.

Evangelicals have frequently pointed out Russell's rationalistic bias against the doctrines of eternal punishment and the Trinity. What is likely to disturb evangelicals, however, is to find that Russell's bias was so much a part of his culture that not even the evangelicals of his day were immune to it. As has been pointed out, some strains of the Calvinistic or Reformed faith in America in Russell's day (and long before him) tended to be rationalistic. The same tendency affected other evangelicals and the general culture at large. Nor are evangelicals entirely free from rationalistic tendencies today. The desire to comprehend God is apparently too universal and too ingrained in humanity for anyone to claim absolute freedom from it.

I do not mean that Russell was *no more* rationalistic than evangelicals in his day. Nor do I mean that since everyone is rationalistic to some degree no one can be blamed for it. My point is rather the reverse. The impulse to take an overly simplistic or reductionistic view of God and his relationship to us is a sinful one. (By reductionistic I mean viewing some reality as less than it really is, thus making it accessible or understandable.) Though this impulse is widespread (if not universal) in sinful humanity, in some cases it becomes a dominant presupposition to which everything else is subordinated. In my estimation this was so in the case of Charles Taze Russell. For him human rationality functioned as an authority over the Bible, dictating what was and was not possible for God to be and do.

Jehovah's Witnesses and God's Incomprehensibility

That Jehovah's Witnesses assume the same rationalistic stance toward the teachings of the Bible as did Russell is fairly easy to show. Jehovah's Witnesses today consistently base their arguments against the doctrines of eternal punishment and the Trinity as much or more on their being unreasonable as on their being unscriptural. This is not to deny that they produce a large battery of arguments that appeal to the Bible in support of their views. However, on close inspection most of these biblically oriented arguments turn out to approach the Bible with the very rationalistic presupposition that is revealed more directly in their criticism of these doctrines as contrary to reason.

A recent example of this emphasis placed by Jehovah's Witnesses on reason is found in their question-and-answer book *Reasoning from the Scriptures* (the title of which is itself suggestive). In the section on the Trinity, the book states:

> Regarding the Trinity, the Athanasian Creed (in English) says that its members are "incomprehensible." Teachers of the doctrine often state that it is a "mystery." Obviously such a Trinitarian God is not the one that Jesus had in mind when he said: "We worship what we know." (John 4:22, *RS*) Do you really know the God you worship?[5]

The assumption here is that to know God we must be able to comprehend him. Such an assumption is not only unwarranted, it is false, because it denies the great difference between the infinite Creator and the finite creature. It regards knowledge of God as primarily intellectual and therefore requires God to be comprehensible to man. That Jehovah's Witnesses assume such an intellectualist view of the knowledge of God may be illustrated by their translation of John 17:3 in the NWT: "This means everlasting life, their taking in knowledge of you, the only true God, and of the one whom you sent forth, Jesus Christ." *Taking in knowledge* refers to the acquiring of doctrinal knowledge about God, implying that such acquisition is what is essentially involved in knowing God and gaining everlasting life. A more literal rendering (as may be seen from the *KIT* interlinear reading, as well as in virtually every other translation) would be, "This is eternal life, that they may *know you* . . ." (emphasis added). Here it becomes evident that what Jesus is referring to is *personal knowledge* of God, knowledge that in essence involves a personal relationship with God. Of course this will imply some doctrinal knowledge about God as well, but the emphasis is decidedly different. The Jehovah's Witnesses' emphasis on doctrinal study is in their case a simple corollary of their rationalistic approach to faith.

Another passage in the same book appears to contradict this rationalistic assumption by admitting that the biblical teaching that God did not have a beginning is incomprehensible to us. The passage is so important for understanding the way Jehovah's Witnesses think about God that I feel I must quote at length from it. After citing Psalm 90:2 as a proof text for God's not having a beginning, the book contains the following comments:

> *Is that reasonable?* Our minds cannot fully comprehend it. But that is not a sound reason for rejecting it. *Consider examples:* (1) *Time.* No one can point to a certain moment as the beginning of time. And it is a fact that, even though our lives end, time does not. We do not reject the idea of time because there are aspects of it that we do not fully comprehend. Rather, we regulate our lives by it. (2) *Space.* Astronomers find no beginning or ending to space. The farther they probe into the universe, the more there is. They do not reject what the evidence shows; many refer to space as being infinite. The same principle applies to the existence of God. . . . [More examples

are given, one from the incredibly high temperature of the sun at its core, the other from the size of the Milky Way.]

Which is more reasonable—that the universe is the product of a living, intelligent Creator? or that it must have arisen simply by chance from a nonliving source without intelligent direction? Some persons adopt the latter viewpoint because to believe otherwise would mean that they would have to acknowledge the existence of a Creator whose qualities they cannot fully comprehend. . . . Should we really expect to understand everything about a Person who is so great that he could bring into existence the universe, with all its intricate design and stupendous size?[6]

Now, in one sense this passage seems to testify to an appreciation of God's incomprehensibility, and the examples given seem genuinely helpful in showing that it is unreasonable to reject the biblical teaching about God simply because we cannot comprehend him. However, the earlier cited criticism of the incomprehensibility of the Trinity should alert us to the possibility of some subtle difference in this passage's talk about man not comprehending God. A simplistic reading would suggest that the two passages flatly contradict one another; but although they do verbally, and although there is some substantial tension between them as well, I do not think they are actually contradictory.

In the passage about God not having a beginning, it is noteworthy that God is never said to be *eternal*. Jehovah's Witnesses believe that God is eternal only in the sense that he always has existed and always will exist. That is, they believe that God's eternality is simply a matter of endless existence *in time*. Orthodox Christianity, on the other hand, has always maintained (not without occasional dissenters within the church, of course) that God's eternality goes beyond endless existence and is actually a matter of transcendence *above time*. The consequences of this difference are much more far-reaching than may be imagined. It implies that the God worshiped by Jehovah's Witnesses is part of the universe of space and time. This is consistent with the passage quoted above, where time and space are both suggested to be of endless extent. Elsewhere Jehovah's Witnesses have plainly stated that they believe God to have a finite body located somewhere in the heavens,[7] contrary to the orthodox position that God is omnipresent, that is, transcendent over space.[8]

More recently the Society has nuanced its view on this matter somewhat, asserting that Jehovah "does not reside in the physical heavens" but rather has his location in the "spiritual heavens." The doctrine of God's omnipresence is still denied.[9] If anything this is worse, because now the Society's view implies that Jehovah is not present *at all* in the space-time universe. Locking God outside of the universe is no improvement over locking him inside it.

The Jehovah's Witnesses' God is therefore apparently no more infinite than space and time itself, and indeed is less than actually infinite. He is as old as time, and will continue indefinitely or unceasingly as will time, but he is not transcendent over time. As for space, the Witnesses' God is not transcendent over space but is located within space with a body of apparently no unusually large dimensions. Thus temporally (in terms of time) the Witnesses' God is infinite, and spatially (in terms of space) he is finite, not infinite.

The consequence is that for the Jehovah's Witnesses God is no more incomprehensible than the universe of space and time itself. God is either a part of the space-time continuum or is excluded from it, and his being without beginning, while difficult to comprehend, is limited to the apparent infinity of space and time. (I should mention that orthodox Christians generally hold that space and time are finite, that space and time were brought into existence when God created the world; moreover, the astronomical and other scientific evidence now appears to substantiate this position.[10])

Thus Jehovah's Witnesses allow God only a certain kind of incomprehensibility: God may be as incomprehensible as the world, perhaps even in some sense more so (though that does not appear to be their position), but not in a fundamentally different way; God's incomprehensibility is not *qualitatively* different than that of the world. Thus unending existence can be attributed to God, but not triunity.

Ironically, this emphasis on rationality leads Jehovah's Witnesses to embrace positions which are flatly contradictory to one another and involve them ultimately in a kind of irrationality. For instance, Jehovah's Witnesses state repeatedly in their publications that there is only one true God, in contrast to false gods.[11] This one true God, of course, is Jehovah. They also admit that Jesus Christ is rightly designated and honored in Scripture as (at least) a god (and therefore is *not* a false god). But if there is only one true God, and Jesus is a god but not a false god, then logically we must deduce that he is a true God—and therefore that he is Jehovah. Instead of submitting to this quite reasonable conclusion, however, and without showing that the argument rests on false premises or is somehow fallacious, Jehovah's Witnesses respond that Jesus *cannot* be Jehovah and the argument must somehow be faulty, although they cannot specify where it goes wrong. This sort of irrationality is evident throughout their doctrinal system. Thus, Jehovah's Witnesses have traded the proper use of reason as a tool in drawing valid inferences from Scripture for an improper use of reason as a judge of what is and is not possible for God.

6

The Jehovah's Witness Hermeneutical Circle

hat draws people to the Jehovah's Witnesses' beliefs? And what keeps them there? When people adopt a system of belief they generally come to see everything from within that system and therefore find it very difficult to change beliefs. This is as true of Jehovah's Witnesses as anyone else—more so, because Jehovah's Witnesses must study constantly in order to become Witnesses and stay Witnesses. This tendency of a belief system to be self-reinforcing is sometimes called the hermeneutical circle, because one ends up supporting one part of the system by appealing to another part.

In this chapter I wish to highlight some of the factors that are particularly important in bringing persons into the Jehovah's Witnesses' hermeneutical circle and that perpetuate the circle, and offer some critical observations about them.

Why People Become Jehovah's Witnesses

A variety of factors lead people to become interested in the Jehovah's Witnesses and encourage them to embrace the Witnesses' religious system. For the sake of analysis it is helpful to divide these factors into doctrinal and nondoctrinal factors. However, as I hope to show, such a division can be somewhat misleading and thus will have to be qualified.

Doctrinally, of course, many people are attracted to the Jehovah's Witnesses' beliefs for the kinds of reasons given in the previous chapter. Many people intensely dislike the doctrine of hell, and Jehovah's Witnesses regularly heap contempt on it, reserving their strongest condemnation for this belief. If any doctrine attracts people into the Witness fold it is the denial of eternal punishment. Many people are also interested in a doctrine of God which avoids paradox and strict incomprehensibility, and the Jehovah's Witness doctrines about God, Christ, and "holy spirit" are, frankly, easier to understand (on the surface) than the orthodox, evangelical doctrines of the Trinity and the Incarnation. Others are attracted to Jehovah's Witnesses by their teaching that most of the redeemed will live forever on a "paradise earth," and that biblical prophecies point to our generation as the one that will see the end of sin and death and the beginning of paradise. Unfortunately, those attracted to this teaching do not know, as many Jehovah's Witnesses never learn, that the organization has been making this same claim since the 1870s!

While such doctrinal matters do lead many to consider becoming Jehovah's Witnesses, a number of nondoctrinal factors also play a part. Many people are extremely pessimistic about life in this world, and Jehovah's Witnesses deliberately (and, from their standpoint, sincerely) appeal to such pessimism. "Human governments are inherently corrupt and evil," say Jehovah's Witnesses, "and will never change; therefore, the only hope for mankind is God's government, which is due to take over any day now. Therefore, stop trying to change society and join us in calling others to wait for God's government to create a new society." Here we see the interplay of doctrinal and nondoctrinal factors; in truth, they are inseparable. The point is that people who respond positively to this message are already predisposed to respond that way by their own feelings about the society in which they live.

Another factor which makes the Jehovah's Witnesses appealing to many is their strong denunciation of Christendom, by which they mean all professing Christian churches and groups besides their own. Many people are disillusioned and even bitter toward Christian churches and religion generally, and Jehovah's Witnesses share those feelings. Often, these feelings toward the churches are justified. Many large segments of Christendom do not uphold the Bible as the word of God. Even in circles where the Bible is recognized as God's word, scandals involving famous leaders (such as televangelists), patently unbiblical teachings and practices, disunity, and sometimes simple lack of friendliness toward strangers drive people away. Most Christian churches have encouraged their members to participate in war, even when this meant killing members of one's own church on the other side. By contrast, Jehovah's Witnesses appear to be a quiet group that is relatively free of scandals, offers biblical warrant for everything it does, is extremely unified, and is eager to incorporate strangers into their fold. And Jehovah's Witnesses roundly condemn all participation in war.

Again, these factors do not prove that Jehovah's Witnesses' beliefs are right and evangelicals' beliefs are wrong, or that Jehovah's Witnesses are justified in rejecting evangelicalism. For one thing, appearances in this case can be deceiving. Space permits only some general observations of relevance. The Jehovah's Witnesses have suffered scandals throughout their history, some exaggerated by outsiders (always the case with scandals), but scandalous nonetheless. The distinctive teachings and practices of the Witnesses, even on minor issues, are not at all biblical. In their relatively short history (little more than a century since the first issue of the *Watchtower* magazine), there have been several schisms, and what unity exists within the Watchtower organization is gained by sheer hierarchical control; what they have is uniformity more than unity.

Finally, it is characteristic of newer, smaller sects, especially those based on antagonism toward culture and society in general, for the people to be extremely friendly toward prospective converts and to go out of their way to encourage new members. That this is so in the case of Jehovah's Witnesses provides no evidence of spirituality or Christian character.

The matter of participation in war is more complex, and indeed the best thing that can be said here is that Jehovah's Witnesses refuse to face the complexities of the Bible's teaching on war and opt for an overly simplistic position. This is consistent with what has already been said about Jehovah's Witnesses preferring simple, easy-to-understand answers. Evangelical Christians have written much on the subject, and a study of these writings would help Jehovah's Witnesses to see that the issue is far more complex than they have realized.[1] Moreover, even those Christians who hold to noncombatant or pacifist positions do not regard all other Christians as automatically apostate or false believers on that account. Christians generally realize that the issue is too complex to warrant condemning people who come to a different understanding of the biblical teaching.

Another nondoctrinal factor that is very influential in encouraging people to become Jehovah's Witnesses is the methodical, well-structured, thorough way in which prospects and members are instructed in the beliefs of the religion, and the corresponding fact that all Jehovah's Witnesses in good standing know what they believe and are able to explain and even defend their beliefs with proof texts from the Bible. Most Christian churches, including evangelical churches, do not instruct their members so well. Many evangelicals are unsure of what they believe on various minor points of doctrine, and even more are unable to state clearly or accurately what they believe; still more are unable to defend their beliefs with any confidence. Thus, for people who are looking for clear, simple, straightforward answers, who want to be confident they have all the answers—or at least all the important answers—the Jehovah's Witnesses' religion can be very appealing.

Yet, once again, what appears from the Jehovah's Witnesses' standpoint to be proof of their divine approval must appear from an evangelical perspective to be proof of the opposite. Certainly evangelical leaders and teachers (such as I) wish that rank-and-file evangelicals were better educated in their beliefs and better able to represent and defend evangelical Christianity. However, unlike the Jehovah's Witnesses, we evangelicals do not think that people's salvation depends on their having a complete grasp on their doctrinal beliefs. Jehovah's Witnesses are taught that gaining "accurate knowledge" on all the areas on which the organization has taken a position is essential if they are to be sure of everlasting life. That is why all active Jehovah's Witnesses are so well-taught; they have to be! Evangelical Christians do not regard gaining accurate doctrinal knowledge as *unimportant;* indeed, many Christians sin in this matter by not pursuing such knowledge to the extent that they are able. But mastering their doctrinal system is not essential to their salvation. The essence of the Christian life is knowing and obeying the true God by faith, not memorizing doctrines and proof texts. Evangelicals need to do more in this area, but the imbalance is really on the Jehovah's Witnesses' side.

The factors which lead people to become Jehovah's Witnesses are therefore at best ambiguous in terms of their biblical basis. This is often the case regardless of the religion under consideration. Many, many people are attracted to evangelical beliefs initially for similarly ambiguous or questionable reasons. Thus, the more important question is whether these beliefs are actually biblical, rather than what attracts people to them initially. The point in identifying these initial factors is to help Jehovah's Witnesses reflect more critically and insightfully into their own religious commitments. Most Jehovah's Witnesses appear to assume that they became Jehovah's Witnesses because they studied the Bible and discovered that the Witnesses' beliefs were biblical. While study of the Bible (through the Watchtower literature) is always a part of a Jehovah's Witness's experience before being baptized as a Witness, it is not necessarily the most important part. Its significance rather is in leading prospective Witnesses to restructure their specific belief system in response to those features of Witness religion to which they were attracted initially.

Why People Remain Jehovah's Witnesses

Once people become Jehovah's Witnesses, a large number of factors reinforce their beliefs and encourage them to remain where they are. All of the factors just discussed in relation to becoming Jehovah's Witnesses continue to maintain them in their beliefs. The authority of the organization and the NWT version of the Bible conformed to Jehovah's Witness beliefs are two additional factors that have been discussed in previous chapters.

The authority of the organization is particularly important. Its claim to speak exclusively and authoritatively for God in the world today works to overcome any doubts Jehovah's Witnesses might have about their beliefs with fear that such doubts are from the devil and may result in their losing out on everlasting life. Jehovah's Witnesses need to realize that it is not a sin to doubt the words of mere men; it is only a sin if the words are actually God's word *itself.*

For example, suppose my pastor says that the Bible teaches that divorce is always wrong, no matter what. It is not wrong for me to doubt my pastor. However, what if I study the Bible on the matter and come to the conclusion that the Bible does indeed teach what my pastor said? The right response is to agree wholeheartedly, without any doubts, with what the Bible says. If I think, "Well, the Bible does say that, but I don't see how that can be right," then I *am* doubting God's word, and that is sin. Later I may study the issue further and realize that the Bible does not actually teach such a view on divorce. (As a matter of fact, I am convinced, as are Jehovah's Witnesses and most evangelicals, that the Bible does allow divorce in certain circumstances; but my illustration does not depend on the accuracy of my opinion here.) *Then* it is right for me to disagree with my pastor, even though I used to be convinced that his interpretation of the Bible on this matter was correct.

Jehovah's Witnesses would be better off taking this approach to the teachings of their leaders. To base unity on treating fallible men as infallible is to base unity on a lie.

The authority of the organization reinforces Witnesses in their beliefs in other, more obvious ways. Jehovah's Witnesses are constantly reminded in their publications and orally by their leaders to remain faithful. They are discouraged from reading religious literature other than their own, and are forbidden to read literature by "apostates." They are warned that if they leave the organization they will be shunned by family members and friends who remain Witnesses. These factors make it very difficult for Jehovah's Witnesses to act on any doubts they may have about the Society's claims to teach the truth.[2]

Doctrinally, the Jehovah's Witnesses' beliefs tend to be self-reinforcing on two levels. The first level I would characterize as the *primary doctrinal system.* This is the system of interlocking doctrinal beliefs that constitutes the Jehovah's Witnesses' main belief structure, their view of God and the world. These doctrines are interdependent and thus both rely on each other and serve to reinforce each other. Beginning where Charles Taze Russell began—the denial of eternal punishment—it is possible to see how all major doctrines of the Jehovah's Witnesses interrelate, as follows:

There is no hell,

Because death is annihilation. But if that is so,

Jesus cannot be God, because Jesus died, and God cannot be annihilated.

Therefore the Trinity is false. But if that is so,

The Holy Spirit must not be a divine person.

Moreover, if Jesus was annihilated, there is no reason to expect that his body would be raised from the dead.

Thus we may conclude that Jesus was raised as a spirit.

But this implies that Jesus will not return physically to the earth.

Therefore, his second advent will be a spiritual presence rather than a physical return.

This allows his second presence to be understood to be happening at this time, unseen except to those who have spiritual insight.

Moreover, if Jesus is a spirit and is to remain forever in heaven, and yet the Bible teaches both that there will be a bodily resurrection and that some will live with Christ and share his nature, that implies that there will be two classes of the redeemed—an earthly class and a heavenly class.

If there is a heavenly class as well as an earthly class, then it follows that the requirements for admission to one class will be somewhat different from the requirements for admission to the other.

Therefore, it makes sense to say that admission to the earthly class requires works in addition to faith and is basically a matter of proving oneself worthy, whereas admission to the heavenly class as a higher privilege is based solely on God's choice—with the qualification that members of the heavenly class all fulfill the requirements for membership in the earthly class.

This explains why some parts of the Bible speak of salvation as requiring obedience and good works, while others speak of everlasting life with God as a free gift.

From this somewhat simplified presentation it should be clear that to challenge any one of these beliefs will have to be perceived as a challenge, at least indirectly, to the whole system. Thus, whenever confidence in one part of the system is challenged, the Jehovah's Witnesses' confidence in the rest of the system bolsters their confidence in the part under attack.

Lest this interlocking character of Watchtower belief be seen as sinister, it should be noted that any decent belief system (humanly speaking) will have a similar structure. Certainly the evangelical system of doctrine can be shown to have a similar internal interdependence. Such a structure is unavoidable in any system of thought which is even moderately self-consistent. A loose collection of independent beliefs that did not affect each other would not provide believers with an integrated way of thinking about their own lives.

Such interdependence among beliefs is a problem, then, only when the system as a whole is false and the person adhering to the system is unwilling to re-examine the system as a whole or any of its parts. The value in pointing out the interlocking structure of Jehovah's Witness beliefs, then, is in making them more sensitive to the need to re-examine all of these beliefs on the basis of Scripture. If even one of these major doctrinal beliefs can be shown to be in serious tension with the Bible, Jehovah's Witnesses ought to consider seriously the possibility that the whole system is faulty.

On the other hand, the interdependence is not a matter of logical necessity in every case. Certainly if death is absolute annihilation, and if Jesus died, Jesus cannot be God; here logical necessity is a feature of the interdependence of these doctrines. If Jesus' second advent is taking place now, it is necessarily a spiritual, invisible presence. But the reverse does not follow. Even if Jesus' second advent is spiritual, it is not necessarily happening now.

The second level of doctrinal reinforcement is what I call the *secondary doctrinal matters*. These are doctrines of the Jehovah's Witnesses that do not tie into the primary doctrinal system and could be altered or dropped without any logical impact on the primary system. Yet, their importance is such that for many Jehovah's Witnesses if these secondary doctrines are suspect the whole religion is suspect.

The kinds of doctrines I have in mind here are especially the Jehovah's Witness "don'ts": blood transfusions, war, participation in political affairs, various celebrations (Christmas, Easter, Thanksgiving, birthdays), the use of the cross as a religious symbol, and the like. On most or all of these issues Jehovah's Witnesses have changed or reversed their earlier positions, with no appreciable impact on their belief system generally. Yet many people are attracted to the Witnesses because of one or more of these "don'ts," and thus would feel even more challenged by criticisms of these doctrines than of the Witness rejection of the Trinity, for instance.

Because the Jehovah's Witnesses are typically alone in their views on these matters, their distinctive position is regarded by Witnesses as further evidence that they have "the truth." If the Bible forbids blood transfusions, they reason, and if we Jehovah's Witnesses are the only ones who recognize this, then obviously we must be blessed by God with the truth. Thus many Jehovah's Witnesses remain confident about their views on God and Christ, even when they are soundly refuted by evangelical apologists, because they know they are right about not celebrating birthdays and Christmas!

There is another way that such beliefs are reinforced, and again the example of blood transfusions is instructive. Through testimonies published in the Watchtower literature and news-type articles published in *Awake!* magazine, Jehovah's Witnesses learn to interpret virtually everything that happens in a way that reinforces rather than challenges their beliefs. When AIDS is reported to have infected the blood supply, this is taken as evidence that blood transfusions themselves are immoral. When patients die from blood transfusions for any reason, a similar conclusion is drawn. When a Jehovah's Witness lives after refusing blood transfusion, this is taken as proof that God blessed his or her integrity. If the Witness dies, this is seen as proof that Jehovah's Witnesses value obedience to God more than their own lives. When medical researchers develop alternatives to blood transfusions, this is cited as evidence that the Jehovah's Witness stand has advanced human knowledge.

As convincing as such interpretations must seem to Jehovah's Witnesses, they find such explanations on similar issues by other religious groups completely unconvincing. A similar structure of reinforcement could be developed, for example, for the Christian Science belief that all sickness and disease should be healed by faith apart from medical procedures. Whenever someone dies in a hospital, this is taken as evidence that faith alone heals; whenever a Christian Scientist recovers apart from medicine, a similar conclusion is drawn; whenever a Christian Scientist dies, he or she is said not to have truly believed; and so on.

The point, then, is that Jehovah's Witnesses, like everybody else (evangelicals included), tend to interpret everything that happens or could happen (within certain limits) as fitting their beliefs. Realizing this should drive all of us back to the Bible to make sure that we have read it correctly. Realizing how easily we rationalize everything that happens to fit our beliefs should foster in us some much-needed humility concerning beliefs we have taken for granted. I make this point especially for the benefit of Jehovah's Witnesses, because I believe their need is particularly acute. But we all need to pay attention.

Finally, Jehovah's Witnesses attend meetings more frequently than most churchgoers; three times a week is fairly common. Most also talk with several people about their beliefs each week, nearly always are in control of the conversation, and feel more knowledgeable about the Bible than the people with whom they speak. This is important, because the more a person hears others saying something and the more he says it himself, the more convinced he becomes of its truth.

I have only been able to touch on some of the most significant ways in which Jehovah's Witnesses are reinforced in their beliefs. At this point it is important to apply some of these observations about Jehovah's Witness hermeneutics to the interpretation of Scripture. In the next chapter I shall discuss one biblical text in which a great many Jehovah's Witness interpretive weaknesses are exemplified.

Case Study in Watchtower Interpretation: *Luke 23:43*

How do Jehovah's Witnesses really interpret the Bible? What assumptions do they make, and what methods do they use? In this chapter I shall analyze the way the Witnesses interpret one short verse of Scripture, Luke 23:43, and the arguments they offer in defense of their interpretation. This analysis will illustrate ten principles of interpretation they regularly violate in their handling of Scripture. These ten principles were all discussed in some form in the first chapter of this book.

The Commotion over a Comma

Luke 23:43 in the NWT reads, "And he [Jesus] said to him [the repentant thief]: 'Truly I tell you today, You will be with me

97

in Paradise.'" Most translations have something like the following for Jesus' words: "Truly I say to you, today you will be
with me in paradise." In other words, the only substantial
point of disagreement is whether *today* belongs with *truly I
say to you* or with *you will be with me in paradise.* To put it
another way, what the fuss is all about is the position of the
comma after instead of before the word *today.*

This may seem unimportant, but it is crucial for the Jehovah's Witnesses to translate it as they have to support their
doctrinal position. Like some other groups, the Witnesses
believe that at death human beings cease to exist as persons.
That is, they deny that there is an immaterial soul or spirit
which can exist as a personal being apart from the body. Their
position is contradicted by Jesus' promise to the thief that he
would be with him in a spiritual paradise that very day. By
changing the position of the comma, *today* is placed with *truly
I say to you,* and thus the idea that Jesus and the thief went
to paradise immediately after their deaths is eliminated.

Before proceeding to criticize their interpretation of this
text, it is appropriate to notice the hermeneutical dynamics
involved. The Jehovah's Witnesses' denial of the soul's personal existence apart from the body is part of their primary
doctrinal system (see chapter 6). Therefore, in challenging
their interpretation of this one text I am in fact challenging
their whole system of religious thought, and therefore their
entire way of life. Evangelicals need to realize that there is
much more going on under the surface than a controversy
over the translation of one particular verse in the Bible.

Where the comma should be placed cannot be determined
by looking for a comma in the Greek text. In ancient Greek
there were no punctuation marks; indeed, all words were run
together with no spaces between them and using all capital
letters.

It might seem, then, that there is no way to prove which
translation is correct, so that the NWT rendering is a legitimate possibility. However, such is not the case, as this chapter will show. And this leads me to my first observation about
Jehovah's Witness interpretation. Jehovah's Witnesses regu-

larly assume that if their translation is grammatically possible, it cannot be criticized. More generally, *Jehovah's Witnesses seek to justify the interpretation that fits their doctrine instead of seeking to know the interpretation which best fits the text.* By no means are they alone in this error, but it is an error to which they are continually prone. This is a general observation that for its validity depends on a careful study of Jehovah's Witnesses' argumentation in defense of their controversial interpretations. Some of the rather forced interpretations of biblical passages discussed earlier in this book might also be cited as examples in this regard.

There is more to interpreting the Bible (or any other text, for that matter) correctly than coming up with a grammatically possible translation. In this case, there are other considerations which decisively prove the usual translation correct and the NWT rendering wrong.

"Amen I Say to You"

A more literal translation than "Truly I tell you" is "Amen I say to you" (in Greek, *Amēn soi legō).* This is an expression or formula used only by Jesus to introduce a truth that is very important and perhaps hard to believe. (In the Gospel of John it is "Amen, amen I say to you.") In its form and usage it is rather like the Old English expression "Hear ye!" A more biblical example is the Old Testament "Thus says the Lord." One biblical scholar has pointed out that "Amen I say to you" emphasized that what Jesus said had divine authority (his own) just as "Thus says the Lord" emphasized that what the prophets said had God's authority.[1] This suggests that "Amen I say to you today" would be just as unlikely an expression as "Thus says the Lord today" or "Hear ye today!" would be.

In fact, seventy-three of the seventy-four times the expression occurs in the Bible, the NWT places a break immediately after it; Luke 23:43 is the only exception. (Most translations follow this pattern in all seventy-four instances.) It does this in two ways. In ten instances the NWT has the word *that* imme-

diately after the expression, so that the text reads, "Truly I
tell you that . . ." (Matt. 5:18; 16:28; 19:23; 21:31; 24:34;
Mark 3:28; 11:23; 12:43; 13:30; Luke 4:24). In sixty-three
instances, the NWT inserts a comma immediately after the
expression and capitalizes the following word (Matt. 5:26;
6:2, 5, 16; 8:10; 10:15, 23, 42; 11:11; 13:17; 17:20; 18:3, 13,
18; 19:28; 21:21; 23:36; 24:2, 47; 25:12, 40, 45; 26:13, 21,
34; Mark 8:12; 9:1, 41; 10:15, 29; 14:9, 18, 25, 30; Luke
11:51; 12:37; 18:17, 29; 21:32; John 1:51; 3:3, 5, 11; 5:19,
24, 25; 6:26, 32, 47, 53; 8:34, 58; 10:1, 7; 12:24; 13:16, 20,
21, 38; 14:12; 16:20, 23; 21:18).

Unless there is overwhelming evidence from the context
that Luke 23:43 is an exception to the above pattern, it
should be translated according to Jesus' normal usage of the
expression. This leads me to my second observation:
Jehovah's Witnesses usually interpret a biblical text deduc-
tively based on their doctrinal system rather than inductively
based on the particulars of the text. That is, they usually base
their interpretation on what they have already concluded
must be true (what I am somewhat simplistically calling
deductive reasoning) rather than examining all of the relevant
material in Scripture before drawing a conclusion (what I
mean by inductive reasoning).

That this is so may be seen by looking for any thorough
studies of individual biblical texts in the publications of the
Watchtower. Such a search will prove rather fruitless; such
studies are virtually nonexistent. For example, the treatment
given in this very chapter of Luke 23:43 is by the standards of
Christian scholarship a study of modest length, but it is much
longer than any treatment of *any* single biblical text I have
seen in Watchtower literature. Among the longest studies of
individual passages of Scripture I have seen are the appendices in the 1984 reference edition of the NWT, and even these
are quite short and very one-sided. Generally Watchtower
publications simply assert that a biblical text has a certain
meaning, and give very little if any careful consideration of
its specific language or immediate written context.

Ideally, our interpretation of Scripture should integrate sound deductive reasoning with solidly based inductive reasoning as well. That is, our interpretations should be consistent with one another and with our doctrinal system, as well as take into full account all of the particular features of the biblical text. The Jehovah's Witnesses' interpretation is long on deductive consistency (though often on closer examination lacking even such consistency) and short on inductive study of the text.

The Position of *Today*

In the Greek text, Luke places *today* (*sēmeron*) immediately after "Amen I say to you." Had he wanted it to be understood as part of Jesus' opening expression, he could have written, "Amen today I say to you" or "Amen I say to you today that" (by adding the word *hoti*, "that"). These wordings would have been capable of being understood only as the Jehovah's Witnesses interpret Luke 23:43. Since the expression "Amen I say to you" regularly stands apart from everything that follows it, the fact that he used neither of these alternative wordings confirms that he meant *today* to be part of what follows.

This illustrates a third point: *Jehovah's Witnesses typically do not consider whether their interpretation best fits the precise wording of the text.* This point closely relates to the previous point about their not basing their interpretation on the particulars of the text. They are generally interested only in choosing an interpretation that if possible does not obviously contradict the text and which is in keeping with their doctrinal position. Examples again are rather easy to come by; most of the misinterpretations discussed earlier in this study qualify.

A footnote in the 1984 Reference Edition of the NWT points out that the Curetonian Syriac version (a fifth-century A.D. translation of the New Testament) "renders this text: 'Amen, I say to thee to-day that with me thou shalt be in the Garden of Eden.'"[2] Ironically, this is evidence not in favor of the NWT punctuation but against it. As Bruce Metzger, the famed

Princeton Greek scholar, has explained, the Syriac version actually "rearranges the order of words" and thereby changes the meaning.[3]

My fourth observation is this: *Jehovah's Witnesses often regard unusual variations or ancient versions as supporting their incorrect renderings, when if anything they constitute evidence against them.* The most outstanding example of this sort of error is the appeal by Jehovah's Witnesses to medieval Hebrew translations of the New Testament which often substitute *YHWH* ("Yahweh" or "Jehovah") for "Lord" in passages quoting from the Old Testament.[4] Only by a tortured line of reasoning can fourteenth-century Hebrew translations of the Greek New Testament be considered as evidence that the original Greek contained the divine name Yahweh in any form. I shall have more to say about this subject in chapter 8.

The Significance of *Today*

Jehovah's Witnesses reason that by saying "truly I tell you *today*" Jesus was emphasizing that his promise to the thief came on a day when the faith in Jesus exhibited by the thief was amazing.[5] Although this sounds plausible, there is no evidence for this explanation in the immediate context. The text makes no reference to the thief's faith, nor is anything else stated that would support this interpretation.

The orthodox interpretation understands the significance of *today* to be that while the thief asked for a place in Jesus' future material kingdom (verse 42), Jesus offered a place with him that very day in a spiritual paradise (verse 43). This view ties directly into the immediate context, and so is to be preferred.

This illustrates a fifth point: *Jehovah's Witnesses often abuse the concept of "context" by broadening it to include their hypothetical reconstructions of how a statement was understood originally, rather than basing their interpretation on the immediate written context.* In my opinion this is one of the most overlooked interpretive errors of Jehovah's Witnesses.

Another interesting example concerns their interpretation of Nebuchadnezzar's dream about a tree chopped down and its stump banded for seven years (Dan. 4:10–17). The Jehovah's Witnesses interpret this dream to symbolize 2520 (7 x 360) years of Gentile domination on the earth unopposed by any earthly theocratic government, beginning with the overthrow of the Davidic throne (which they date in 607 B.C.) and ending with the supposed beginning in A.D. 1914 of Christ's invisible rule over the earth through his "theocratic organization" on earth, the Jehovah's Witnesses.[6] Although every aspect of this interpretation invites criticism, the point to which I wish to draw attention is a rather simple one. The Witnesses argue that the dream had to give information about the end times because that is a major theme of the Book of Daniel.[7] This implicit appeal to context, however, virtually dictates to the Book of Daniel what sorts of visions it may report. Moreover, in the immediate context Daniel interprets the dream as fulfilled in Nebuchadnezzar himself, which the Witnesses briefly acknowledge but do not find satisfying. In fact, the significance of the dream is that the seven years represent a period of interruption in this Gentile king's rule. In other words, the Jehovah's Witnesses' interpretation depends on their claim that a period of seven years in which a Gentile king *did not* rule represents a period of 2520 years during which Gentile kings *did* rule. Thus their appeal to the larger context of Daniel, while it lends seeming plausibility to their argument, is made irrelevant by a consideration of the actual teaching of the passage itself. This sort of error occurs with surprising frequency in Watchtower literature, and I have listened to Jehovah's Witnesses commit this error even more frequently in personal conversation.

Paradise

The word *paradise* in biblical times had a varied history. In the Septuagint, the Greek translation of the Old Testament used by Greek-speaking Jews in the first century, the word referred to the Garden of Eden (Gen. 2:8–10), as well as to a

future transformation of Israel's land to resemble the Garden
of Eden (Isa. 51:3; Ezek. 36:35). However, in first-century
A.D. Judaism *paradise* referred primarily to a "hidden" place
of blessedness for the righteous between the time of their
death and the future resurrection. This is the usage reflected
in Jesus' reference to paradise in Luke 23:43.[8]

To show that this was not the Jewish understanding in
Jesus' day, the Jehovah's Witnesses quote *The New International Dictionary of New Testament Theology*: "With the infil-
tration of the Gk. [Greek] doctrine of the immortality of the
soul paradise becomes the dwelling-place of the righteous
during the intermediate state."[9] However, in context this reference work is saying that the idea of an intermediate paradise for the dead developed in Judaism after the Old Testament period and was the Jewish view in Jesus' day. It goes on
to state, "In Lk. 23:43 it [the word *paradise*] is no doubt dependent on contemporary Jewish conceptions, and refers to the
at present hidden and intermediate abode of the righteous."[10]

In at least three different discussions of Luke 23:43, the
Jehovah's Witnesses cite James Hastings's *Dictionary of the
Bible* to prove that there is "little support" for the "theory"
that first-century Judaism conceived of an intermediate paradise.[11] What Hastings actually says is this: "It is certain that
the belief in a *lower* Paradise prevailed among the Jews, as
well as the belief in an *upper* or heavenly Paradise." On the
same page he also states regarding Luke 23:43 that "Christ
referred to the Paradise of heaven."[12]

These two examples of misuse of biblical scholarship illustrate my sixth point: *Jehovah's Witnesses often cite scholarly
sources selectively and out of context, usually to support a
conclusion opposite to that supported by the source.* It is one
thing to show that a scholarly source provides evidence for
one's position despite its reaching a different conclusion; that
is legitimate, but that is not what the Jehovah's Witnesses
have done. Rather, they have quoted from the scholarly work
in a way designed to give the misleading impression that the
source reaches the same conclusion as they do. This happens
all too often in Watchtower publications. Many evangelical

publications, including some by this author, have documented examples of this kind of error,[13] so I will not belabor the point here with additional examples.

The only other places in the New Testament the word *paradise* occurs are Revelation 2:7 and 2 Corinthians 12:4, and both are instructive. The Jehovah's Witnesses themselves state that the "paradise of God" in Revelation 2:7 is a heavenly paradise, though they do not recognize it as an intermediate state for the dead between their death and resurrection.[14]

Second Corinthians 12:4 is even more interesting. The parallel between "paradise" and "the third heaven" indicates that paradise here is a heavenly realm, as nearly all biblical scholars commenting on the passage have recognized. Indeed, paradise was said to be in the third heaven in Jewish literature circulating in the first century.[15]

The Jehovah's Witnesses, however, have argued that Paul was referring to "a spiritual state among God's people" during "the time of the 'harvest season'" which would come just prior to the End.[16] In other words, they claim that Paul had a vision of the Jehovah's Witnesses of today! Of the many objections to this interpretation, we may mention just two: Nothing in the context of 2 Corinthians 12 hints that paradise is the people of God in the last days; and if paradise there means God's people, then so does the third heaven, which is absurd.

The Jehovah's Witnesses' handling of 2 Corinthians 12:4 illustrates a seventh observation: *Jehovah's Witnesses frequently allegorize prophecies and visions in Scripture to make them refer to events in the history of the Jehovah's Witnesses, always with no basis in the text itself.* A study of the Jehovah's Witnesses' recent commentary on Revelation will provide many illustrations of this interpretive abuse of Scripture.[17]

"With Me"

Jesus promised the thief, "You will be *with me* in paradise." This statement contradicts the Jehovah's Witnesses' doctrine in two ways. First, "You will be with me" implies that all believers in Christ will live in his presence, whereas Jehovah's Witnesses believe that most believers will live on the earth while a select few will live in heaven with Christ. Second, "with me in paradise" implies that Christ went to paradise, whereas Jehovah's Witnesses teach that paradise will be on earth and Christ will stay in heaven.

The Jehovah's Witnesses explain, ". . . he will be with that man in the sense that He will raise him from the dead and care for his needs, both physical and spiritual."[18] However, in other places where Jesus speaks of others being "with me" (Luke 22:28; Rev. 3:21; see also Rev. 14:1; 20:4, 6), the Jehovah's Witnesses take it literally.[19] There is no good reason not to do so also in Luke 23:43.

This is a good example of my eighth observation: *Jehovah's Witnesses are often forced to interpret simple expressions in highly figurative fashion, with no warrant from the context, to maintain their doctrinal position.* Another from among many possible examples is the Witness argument that when Jesus said, "Break down this temple, and in three days I will raise it up" (John 2:19), he did not mean that he would raise himself from the dead, but only that he would provide God with the "moral basis" for his resurrection.[20] "I will" thus is interpreted to mean (with no basis in the context itself) "God will because of what I have done." Yet another example comes from this same passage: Although John tells us that by "temple" Jesus meant "his body" (John 2:21), Jehovah's Witnesses usually take "his body" figuratively to refer to the church (or "Christian congregation," as they put it). These two fanciful interpretations are necessitated by their unwillingness to acknowledge that Jesus is God and that he rose bodily from the grave.

Where Did Christ Go?

When Jesus died, the Bible indicates, he went initially down into Hades, even down into the "abyss" (Matt. 12:40; Acts 2:27, 31; Rom. 10:7; Eph. 4:9; Rev. 1:18). How, then, could

he promise the thief that they would be together in a heavenly paradise? Did he not tell Mary after his resurrection that
he had "not yet ascended to the Father" (John 20:17)? The
Jehovah's Witnesses argue that these facts are incompatible
with the orthodox interpretation of Luke 23:43.

Before responding to this argument, it should be noted
what the Jehovah's Witnesses are doing here. Instead of dealing with Luke 23:43 on its own terms and in its own context
(which, as we have seen, they cannot do and maintain their
beliefs), they argue that Luke 23:43 *cannot* mean what it
appears to mean because that would contradict their understanding of other biblical passages. Now, in one sense this
may be taken positively as an indication of the Jehovah's
Witnesses' commitment to the absolute truthfulness of all
Scripture. No doubt they would insist that this is what is at
stake. However, what is in fact being done is that the
Witnesses are "saving" the Bible from contradiction by mis-
interpreting it. That is, they are implying that the Bible as it
stands *is* contradictory, so that it cannot be taken at face
value even after all the particular features of the wording and
context are taken into consideration.

In short, *Jehovah's Witnesses pit one part of Scripture
against another part to force the Bible to agree with their
doctrine.* This is one of the most frequent errors of Jehovah's
Witness biblical interpretation. John 14:28 is said to rule out
the possibility that John 1:1 makes Jesus God, regardless of
the particular language used in John 1:1 (and indeed, without careful consideration of the precise language and context
of John 14:28). In personal dialogue with Jehovah's
Witnesses I have seen this error committed repeatedly. One
rather naive Jehovah's Witness even presented me with a list
of Scriptures "pro" and "con" on the Trinity, with texts such
as John 1:1 listed as "pro" and John 14:28 listed as "con"!

A little digging into the historical usage of the term *paradise* helps to clear up the apparent discrepancy in this case. In
first-century Judaism, the intermediate paradise was sometimes thought of as in heaven per se, but at other times
thought of as a "happy" compartment in Hades.[21] Jesus' words

in Luke 23:43 refer most probably to paradise as a part of Hades for the righteous. That is, Jesus promised the thief that they would be together not in heaven that day but in the blessed resting place of the dead. From 2 Corinthians 12:4 it can be gathered that Christ in effect took paradise to heaven with him when he ascended to heaven.[22]

In putting matters this way we should keep in mind that the heaven which is God's "abode" is not a locality fixed within our space-time universe. The physical heavens cannot contain God (1 Kings 8:27; Isa. 66:1; Acts 7:48–49). Even if we could travel fast enough, we could not find God or his "abode" by searching the stars. Thus, language about where Jesus and the thief went should not be taken literally.

This suggests a tenth point: *Jehovah's Witnesses interpret the spiritual realities spoken of in the Bible in an overly rationalistic manner.* By rationalistic I mean, not expecting the teachings of the Bible to be in accord with sound reason, but demanding that the Bible's teachings always fit man's limited comprehension. Human understanding is finite, but God in his being and in his understanding is infinite. In any matter concerning the essence of God or the relationship between God and his creation we should *expect* paradoxes. The Jehovah's Witnesses' system of doctrine seeks to do away with all paradox. They demand a God they can comprehend.

8

Jehovah's Witnesses and the Divine Name

D o Jehovah's Witnesses understand the Bible correctly? In previous chapters of this book I argued that they do not, giving several examples of their mistranslations and misinterpretations of specific texts of the Bible. But there is more to interpreting the Bible than identifying the meaning of isolated statements here and there. One must understand the Bible's teachings as a whole, its major themes and concerns, if one is to interpret the Bible correctly.

In this final chapter I wish to study an example of how Jehovah's Witnesses handle one of the Bible's major doctrinal themes. The case study I will discuss is the Jehovah's Witnesses' teaching on the divine name in Scripture.

Jehovah or Yahweh?

In this chapter I will disagree strongly with most of what Jehovah's Witnesses have to say about the divine name. However, first I wish to express agreement with them on one issue for which they are often criticized by evangelicals—wrongly, I think. Evangelicals often urge that if Jehovah's Witnesses insist on the use of the divine name they should use the correct form *Yahweh* rather than *Jehovah*. To this criticism the Witnesses have made the following responses.

1. The actual form of the name might have been *Yahweh*, but it might not have been; the original form is not known with certainty. The reason for this uncertainty is that the original Hebrew alphabet had no vowels; thus, the divine name was spelled *YHWH* (in English this could be Anglicized to *JHWH* or *JHVH*). Medieval Jewish scribes added marks called vowel points next to the consonants to aid pronunciation. However, since for centuries Jews had avoided pronouncing the divine name and had instead said *Adonay* whenever they came to *YHWH* in the Hebrew text, the Jewish scribes added the vowel points for *Adonay* (*a-o-a*) to *YHWH*, resulting in *Yahowah* or *Jehovah*. Although scholars are fairly certain that *Yahweh* was the original form, this does not appear to be proved beyond dispute. On the other hand, as the above history proves, and as the Witnesses admit, it is absolutely certain that *Jehovah* was not the original form.[1]

2. All names vary somewhat from language to language; for example, *Jesus* in Hebrew might have been pronounced either *Yeshua* or *Yehoshua*, and in modern languages it varies in form as well.[2] An even more striking example is the fact that *James* in English Bibles translates the Greek *Iakōbos*, that is, *Jacob*.

3. *Jehovah* is now the customary, conventional form in English (and with minor variations in many other languages as well), and as such is the most easily recognizable form of the divine name. Although this is much less true today than it was a century ago, it cannot be denied that the form *Jehovah* is still widely used outside Jehovah's Witness circles.

For these reasons I do not criticize Jehovah's Witnesses for using the form *Jehovah* rather than *Yahweh*. And I would add a fourth, more theological, reason: God does not care about the exact form of the divine name or he would have ensured its preservation. In the rest of this article I shall use the form *Jehovah*; those who prefer may read this as *Yahweh* or *YHWH*.

The Meaning of *Jehovah*

There is no consensus among biblical scholars as to the meaning of *Jehovah*. According to the Jehovah's Witnesses, the divine name "actually signifies 'He Causes to Become.' Thus, God's name identifies Him as the One who progressively fulfills his promises and unfailingly realizes his purposes."[3] Similarly, the phrase in Exodus 3:14 usually translated "I Am Who I Am" (*'ehyeh asher 'ehyeh*) is in the NWT rendered "I Shall Prove To Be What I Shall Prove To Be."

Other scholars have argued for a similar interpretation of the divine name, though the details of the argument differ.[4] The exact interpretation of the name, however, is still a matter of debate, and we need not be concerned here to settle on the one right view. In fact, as I explained in chapter 1, the original or etymological meaning of a word may not necessarily be the meaning the word comes to have over time. In this case it is interesting to note that most of the interpretations which are under serious consideration, if related properly to the biblical view of God, actually imply one another.

Consider these views briefly. One view holds that Jehovah means "He is," meaning that God simply is who he is and cannot be defined because he is greater than the human mind can completely fathom or comprehend. Another view also holds that Jehovah means "He is," but understands this to mean that God is self-existent, that is, eternal and dependent on no one and nothing else for his existence. This is the view reflected in the Septuagint, the Greek translation of the Old Testament used most often by the New Testament writers; it translates Exodus 3:14 "I am the One who is" (*egō eimi ho ōn*).[5] A third view takes Jehovah to mean "He causes to be" and interprets this to mean that God is the Creator—that everything that exists besides God himself was created by God. A fourth view renders Jehovah as "He will become" and takes this to imply that God will do whatever is needed to fulfill his promises; this is essentially the Jehovah's Witnesses' view, and that of others as well.

Whichever of these views is right, the truths about God which they understand the divine name to express all necessarily imply one another. For God to be able to fulfill his incredible promises to his people he must be in complete control of human history and indeed of the whole universe; but this implies that he is the Creator and sustainer of the world. That God is the Creator of the world and the one who can guarantee such amazing promises about matters thousands of years in the future implies that he is not bound by time but is eternal—which implies that he is self-existent. Such an amazing God, who is the Creator and sustainer of all things, who is beyond the restrictions of time, is certainly beyond man's ability to completely or exhaustively comprehend— which implies that he cannot be simply and neatly defined as the pagans labeled their many imaginary gods.

The essence of God's name Jehovah, then, regardless of the precise original meaning of the Hebrew form, is that he is absolutely supreme and in control of everything. In short, the name Jehovah reveals God as *Lord*—Lord of creation, of history, and of his people. It would appear to be no accident, then, and no mistake, that *Lord* has come to take the place of *Jehovah* both in the New Testament and in most translations of the Old Testament. That this conclusion is in fact biblically sound shall be further demonstrated as we consider the biblical teaching about the divine name.

One more point should be noticed: The Jehovah's Witnesses do not really believe in this Lord whose absolute sovereignty is revealed in the name Jehovah. As I explained in chapter 5, Jehovah's Witnesses deny that God is incomprehensible except in the same sense that other wonders of the universe are incomprehensible. They deny that God is strictly speaking eternal, that is, transcendent over time; they maintain rather that God simply has always existed and will continue always to exist. The Jehovah's Witnesses' God is also not omnipresent, but has a body of spirit located at some fixed place (either inside or outside the physical universe). Thus, their "God" is not the absolute Creator of space and time, but is a relative entity either locked into the universe of space and time along with the rest of us, or locked outside of space but existing in time. Ironically, then, the very name about which Jehovah's Witnesses make such a fuss reveals God as being infinitely greater than they admit him to be.

The Necessity of the Name

According to Jehovah's Witnesses, it is essential that God's people use God's name Jehovah regularly when praying to him and talking to others about him. Only the name Jehovah, they argue, applies uniquely to the true God and to no other god. False gods are called God, Lord, and even Father; such *titles*, then, in contrast to God's *name*, are not distinctive designations of the true God.[6]

These arguments, though they seem reasonable to Jehovah's Witnesses, are not biblical. First, it is not true that only the name Jehovah applies uniquely to the true God. For example, the expression "the God of Abraham, God of Isaac, and God of Jacob" serves to identify the true God as well as does the name Jehovah.

Second, the distinction between name and title is not hard and fast in Scripture. In fact there does not seem to be an equivalent word for title, and nowhere does the Bible make this distinction explicit. In Matthew 1:23 we are told that Jesus was to be given the name Immanuel, which of course was not his proper name (see also Isa. 9:6).

Third, the books of Esther and Ecclesiastes never use the name Jehovah, not even once, although Ecclesiastes does use the word *God* (Hebrew, *elohim*) some forty-one times. This suggests that use of the name is not essential in religious matters.

Fourth, the New Testament does not use Jehovah once, but instead regularly uses Lord (or, a few times, God), particularly in its quotations from the Old Testament. Thus the New Testament, at least as it stands, testifies by its lack of the name Jehovah that it is not essential to use it.

Of course, it is the evidence of the New Testament which is most obviously at odds with the Jehovah's Witnesses' teaching on the divine name. Consequently, in their NWT the name Jehovah is used 237 times in the New Testament. Because they know this will strike most people as strange, not to mention improper, they have given considerable attention to justifying this practice. We will need, then, to consider the arguments used by the Witnesses in defense of their "restoring" the name Jehovah to the New Testament.

The Divine Name in the Septuagint

The Septuagint (for which the abbreviation *LXX* is standard) was a translation of the Old Testament from Hebrew into Greek that was produced in the third century B.C., and from which the New Testament frequently quotes. In most versions of the LXX which have come down to us through ancient manuscript copies the word *Lord* (Greek, *kurios*) is used in place of the divine name, and this practice is also followed in all of the thousands of ancient New Testament Greek manuscripts that have survived.

To counter this evidence, Jehovah's Witnesses argue that the divine name was used in the original version of the LXX, and that the versions which used *kurios* were produced sometime after the first century A.D. by apostate scribes. They base this claim on some pre-New Testament manuscripts of the LXX which have been discovered in this century.

The claim that the original LXX used the divine name is not original with the Jehovah's Witnesses. Origen in the third century and Jerome in the late fourth century both held this view (though without drawing the same conclusions as do the Witnesses), and it has been revived in this century by a few biblical scholars.[7]

As shall be explained shortly, it is unnecessary here to discuss the pros and cons of this theory. Several recent studies show there is insufficient evidence to prove that the original LXX used the divine name, though everyone admits that *some* (not many) copies of the LXX did use it. These studies point out that the manuscripts on which the theory is based all contain signs that they were not typical examples of the LXX, and that internal evidence from the LXX itself shows that from the beginning it must have used *kurios* in place of the divine name.[8]

What is important to point out here is that even if the original LXX *did* use the divine name, that would not prove that the New Testament writers must have used it when quoting from the Old Testament, since they did not always follow the LXX exactly even when quoting from it.[9] The reverse, we may add for the Jehovah's Witnesses' benefit, is for the same reason also true: Even if the original LXX did not use the divine name, the New Testament might have done so. Thus whether or not the LXX originally used the divine name, the New Testament might have followed a different practice. The only way we can know what the New Testament writers did is to examine the New Testament itself.

The New Testament and the Divine Name

Thousands of manuscripts of the New Testament (either portions or its entirety) written in Greek, the original language of the New Testament, have been found dating from the second century and later. So far, none of these manuscripts have contained the divine name, as the Witnesses admit.[10] All have regularly used *kurios* in places where the New Testament quotes from or alludes to an Old Testament passage which in the original Hebrew used the divine name. Thus the New Testament, as it has actually been preserved in the manuscripts which have come down to us, definitely does not contain the divine name.

Despite this evidence, Jehovah's Witnesses argue that the New Testament must have originally contained the divine name. They contend, for example, that Matthew wrote his Gospel originally in Hebrew, and would therefore have used the Hebrew name Jehovah in his original Gospel.[11] Although it is *possible* that Matthew wrote an earlier version of his Gospel in Hebrew, that is not certain fact, and no copy of it has survived. Moreover, even if Matthew had used the divine name in a now-lost Hebrew Gospel, that in no way proves that the rest of the New Testament writers must have done the same in their original Greek writings.

Jehovah's Witnesses also appeal to a large number of medieval translations of the New Testament into Hebrew which frequently used the divine name in place of *kurios*.[12] However, since these manuscripts were translated from the Greek and were produced over a thousand years after the New Testament was written, they cannot lend support to the theory that the New Testament originally contained the divine name.[13]

Ultimately, the Jehovah's Witnesses' belief in this matter rests not on these textual considerations but on their understanding of what the New Testament actually has to say about the divine name. Jehovah's Witnesses argue that the practice of using substitutes such as Lord and God for the divine name was a superstitious practice which had developed among the Jews as a way of avoiding taking the name of Jehovah in vain (Exod. 20:7). Jesus, they reason, would not "have followed such an unscriptural tradition," given his forthright condemnation of the Pharisees for their traditions which "went beyond God's inspired Word."[14] Jesus showed his respect for God's name when he taught the disciples to pray, "Let your name be sanctified" (Matt. 6:9 NWT), and by his statement in prayer to the Father, "I have made your name manifest" (John 17:6). They argue on this basis that when Jesus read aloud in the synagogue from Isaiah 61:1–2, which contained the divine name in Hebrew, he must have spoken the divine name rather than a substitute.[15] The apostles are said to have continued

Jesus' teaching on this matter by their speaking of Christians as "a people for His name" (Acts 15:14–15).[16]

This line of reasoning is mistaken at every step. First, the fact is that the practice of substituting Lord or God for the divine name can be traced as far back as the *Old Testament*. For example, Psalm 53 is nearly identical word for word with Psalm 14, but four times substitutes God for Jehovah (Ps. 14:2, 4, 6, 7; 53:2, 4, 5, 6).[17] This one example proves that using substitutes for the divine name is not an "unscriptural practice."

Second, Jesus evidently used various substitutes, as can be seen from passages where he was not quoting the Old Testament. As one biblical scholar explains, "Jesus allows the prodigal son to say, 'Father, I have sinned against heaven and before you' (Luke 15:21), a phrase in which the Name has been replaced by the word 'heaven.' The phrase about seeing the Son of man sitting 'at the right hand of Power' (Matt. 26:64) is another example."[18]

Third, Jesus' references to God's name are striking in that in the immediate context, even in the NWT, neither the name Jehovah nor any substitute is used. Thus, the model prayer which Jesus taught to his disciples addresses God not as Jehovah, but as "our Father" (Matt. 6:9; see also Luke 11:2). Not once in Jesus' long prayer in John 17 does he address God as Jehovah, but always as Father (John 17:1, 11, 21, 24, 25). In these passages God's name evidently stands for his character and reputation; no concern is expressed that Christians use the divine name.

In fact, even with the use of Jehovah in the NWT Jesus appears to have used the divine name very sparingly. In the NWT it occurs in 20 texts reporting the words of Jesus, most of which are quotations from the Old Testament (Matt. 4:4, 7, 10; 5:33; 21:42; 22:37, 44; 23:39; Mark 12:29–30, 36; Luke 4:8, 12, 18–19; 10:27; 13:35; 20:37, 42; John 6:45; the exceptions are Mark 5:19; 13:20). By contrast, Jesus used God over 180 times and Father roughly 175 times.

Fourth, if Jesus had used the divine name in his speech and when reading aloud from the Old Testament, his doing so would have been harshly condemned by the Jews. Yet, while we read of Jesus being condemned repeatedly for his doing work on the Sabbath, contradicting the teachings of the Pharisees, and claiming to be God's Son, we never read of any controversy over his use of the divine name. After he read aloud from Isaiah 61:1–2, the people in the synagogue at Nazareth at first spoke well of Jesus and of his words (Luke 4:22) and were provoked only when Jesus told them that the message of the fulfillment of Isaiah's prophecy was not for them (4:23–30). If he had pronounced the divine name in his reading of the Scripture, his doing so would have provoked an immediate outcry.

Fifth, the apostles' teaching likewise does not show any evidence of concern for the use of the name Jehovah. In Acts 15 when James speaks of a people for God's name, he does not use the name Jehovah (according to the NWT) except when quoting from the Old Testament (Acts 15:17); elsewhere he speaks simply of God (15:14, 19). James's point is not that Christians use the name Jehovah but that they identify themselves with the true God and honor what his name represents.

As I have already explained, the essential significance of the name Jehovah (*YHWH*), whatever its original precise meaning, is that he is Lord. Thus, however the practice of substituting Lord for the divine name arose, in God's sovereign purpose this practice reflected the true significance of his name.

Finally, the claim that the divine name was removed from the New Testament by apostate scribes and an unscriptural substitute put in its place (which contradicts the Bible's own teaching and has no evidence to support it) contradicts one of the Jehovah's Witnesses' own teachings about the Bible. As I noted in chapter 1, Jehovah's Witnesses strongly affirm that the Bible has not been significantly changed through the process of copying and recopying over the centuries. This affirmation is not only factually correct, it is necessarily true if the Bible is to be believed as God's unchanging word (Isa. 40:8; 55:11; Matt. 5:18; John 10:35). To argue that the use of God's name is essential to true Christian faith, and then to claim that for centuries the divine name has been erroneously left out of the Christian Scriptures, is to imply that God failed to preserve his word sufficiently to communicate his essential concerns to mankind. Such an implication undermines confidence not only in the Bible as God's word but in God himself as the sovereign Lord of history. Thus, in this regard also, Jehovah's Witnesses are not faithful to what they have already confessed to be the truth about the Bible.

Jesus and Jehovah

Jehovah's Witnesses deny that Jesus is Jehovah, the true God, maintaining instead that he is a created angel. The *Watchtower* has argued, "If Jesus of the 'New Testament' is Jehovah of the 'Old Testament,' as many claim, should there not at least be one Biblical reference saying that Jesus is Jehovah? Yet there is not one."[19]

Of course, the name Jesus with reference to Christ never appears in the Old Testament, and the name Jehovah in most Bibles never appears in the New Testament (and rightly so). So it is clearly impossible for the Bible to say, in just so many words, that Jesus is Jehovah. On the other hand, the Bible also never says in just so many words that the Father is Jehovah. Although it may seem obvious that the Father is Jehovah, heretical sects throughout history have denied it, including Mormonism, which teaches that Elohim and Jehovah are two separate beings and that the Father is Elohim and Jesus the Son is Jehovah.[20]

The Bible, of course, teaches that Jehovah is the only true *elohim* (Gen. 2:4; Deut. 6:4; Isa. 45:5, 21), that is, the only true God. Jesus calls the Father "God" and "the only true God" (John 6:27; 17:3), thus making it clear that the Father is Jehovah, even though the Bible nowhere *explicitly* says so, and in fact never says that the Father is Lord (though Jesus does address the Father as "Lord of heaven and earth," Matt. 11:25; Luke 10:21).

By the same reasoning, however, Jesus himself must be recognized to be Jehovah. He is identified in Scripture as "the Mighty God" (Isa. 9:6; compare 10:21), as "God" (John 1:1), "my God" (John 20:28), "our great God and Savior" (Titus 2:13; 2 Peter 1:1), and "the true God and eternal life" (1 John 5:20).[21] Moreover, the Bible in more than one place explicitly says, "Jesus is Lord," which is the clearest way the New Testament *could* affirm that Jesus is Jehovah (Rom. 10:9; 1 Cor. 12:3; Phil. 2:11). Elsewhere the New Testament calls Jesus Lord in contexts where it is quoting or paraphrasing Old Testament texts which in Hebrew used the divine name (Heb. 1:10–12; 1 Peter 2:3; 3:15). Moreover, when the apostle Paul uses the expression *one Lord*, it is clear from the context that he always has *Jesus* in mind, even though *one Lord* in the Old Testament means "one Jehovah" (Deut. 6:4).[22]

The Jehovah's Witnesses have attempted to turn this evidence on its head by arguing that the substitution of *Lord* for the divine name in the New Testament resulted in "confusion" between the Lord Jehovah and the Lord Jesus. They have recently found an ally in this claim in one biblical scholar, George Howard, who also supports their claim that the original Septuagint used the divine name.[23]

However, the evidence from the New Testament contradicts the Jehovah's Witnesses' (and Howard's) theory. As has already been noted, the claim that the New Testament originally used the divine name contradicts the manuscript evidence and the teaching of the New Testament. Moreover, it can be shown that if *Jehovah* is substituted for *Lord* in the New Testament selectively to avoid Jesus being called Jehovah, the passages where this is done become incoherent.

For example, in Romans 10:9–13 Paul's argument depends on the *Lord* of verse 13 being the same as the *Lord* of verse 9. These verses are connected by a series of statements beginning with the word *for* (*gar*), meaning "because" or "for this reason": If you confess that Jesus is Lord and believe that God raised him from the dead you shall be saved (vv. 9–10), for (*gar*) no one putting faith in him (Jesus) will be disappointed (v. 11), for (*gar*) there is no distinction between Jew and Greek (v. 12), for (*gar*) the same Lord (Jesus) is over all, rich enough to save all who call on him (v. 12). Then comes a quote from Joel 2:32: "For (*gar*) 'everyone who calls on the name of the Lord will be saved'" (v. 13). This makes perfectly good sense if the Lord of verse 13 is the same as the Lord in verses 9 and 12: Jesus will save both Jew and Gentile, because he is the Lord of all and will save whoever calls on him, as the Scripture itself *says* that whoever calls on the Lord will be saved. However, if Lord in verse 13 means someone entirely different from Lord in verses 9 and 12, the result is nonsense: Jesus will save both Jew and Gentile if they call on him as their Lord, *because* whoever calls on Jehovah (who is someone other than Jesus) will be saved. It makes no sense to say that you should call on Mr. Jones to save you because whoever calls on Mr. Smith will be saved. Yet this is basically the way Jehovah's Witnesses must read Romans 10:9–13: by making the word *Lord* in verse 13 Jehovah the true God and the word *Lord* in verse 9 Jesus a lesser god under Jehovah.

Who Is on Jehovah's Side?

Jehovah's Witnesses take great pride in their constant use of the name Jehovah, even to the point of calling themselves Jehovah's Witnesses. Ironically, the passage of Scripture on which this name is based indicates that they are not faithful witnesses to Jehovah, since it states that the primary truth to which those witnesses were to testify was that Jehovah is the only God and the only Savior (Isa. 43:10–11). By their teaching that Jesus was a created god and a divine savior under Jehovah, the Jehovah's Witnesses prove themselves unfaithful witnesses.

True witnesses to Jehovah will accept the Bible which Jehovah inspired and preserved through the centuries with his message intact (Isa. 40:8; 55:10–11; Matt. 5:18). They will therefore reject the New World Translation, which adds to God's word to change its clear teaching that Jehovah is no longer concerned that we use that name, and makes many other doctrinally significant alterations of God's word (Prov. 30:6).

True witnesses of Jehovah will honor the *meaning* of Jehovah's name, which is that he is the absolute sovereign Lord of all. They will not diminish his greatness by denying that he knows all things, denying that he transcends space and time, or denying that he was able to incarnate himself in Jesus Christ.

True witnesses of Jehovah will follow the teaching of the "faithful and true witness," Jesus Christ (Rev. 3:14), who taught his disciples to be *his* witnesses (Acts 1:8). They will also accept the New Testament teaching that Jesus himself is Jehovah (Rom. 10:9–13; 1 Cor. 12:3; Phil. 2:9–11; Heb. 1:10–12; 1 Peter 2:3; 3:15).

We conclude, then, that Jehovah's Witnesses are not truly on Jehovah's side (Exod. 32:26). Though they mouth his name, they distort his word, diminish his greatness, and deny his incarnation in the Lord Jesus Christ. No clearer proof could be given that Jehovah's Witnesses are unfaithful to God in their interpretation of the Bible.

Conclusion

The Jehovah's Witnesses confess that the Bible is the inerrant word of God. Yet, the way they handle Scripture effectively nullifies this confession. Based on a desire to comprehend God and his dealings with man, Jehovah's Witnesses twist the Scriptures in the way they translate the Bible as well as in the way they interpret it. So difficult is it for people who constantly expose themselves to the text of Scripture to continue believing that the Jehovah's Witnesses' doctrinal system is biblical that the Watchtower Society finds it necessary to remind its people in nearly every issue of the *Watchtower* magazine to remain trustful and uncritically accepting of everything the "faithful and discreet slave" teaches.

It is my hope and prayer that Jehovah's Witnesses reading this study will not merely be shaken in their beliefs, though inevitably some shaking is needed. My hope is that they will be challenged to abandon the unstable foundation of the Watchtower and build their faith on the sure foundation of the Scriptures. In the word of God alone is found unerring truth about God that is both reasonable and beyond the ability of human reason to comprehend. May many Jehovah's Witnesses by God's grace come to know this incomparable and infinitely amazing God.

What Scholars Think of the New World Translation

To counter the frequent criticism that the NWT is an unscholarly translation, the Jehovah's Witnesses often quote various writings which they claim give scholarly approval of the NWT. Although this matter is not directly relevant to this book's concern to understand and critique the way Jehovah's Witnesses read the Bible, it is relevant to evaluating the NWT, and so something should be said about it.

I must first say by way of qualification that the reliability of the NWT does not stand or fall on the opinions of scholarly reviewers. Their opinions are worth considering, and they may very well be right in what they say, but their opinions are not to be treated as infallible (as we have said about scholars in general in chapter 1). The real issue that I wish to consider here is whether the Watchtower publications tell the whole story in their citations of scholarly reviews of the NWT. This is important because the Society claims that it does give the whole story and that it presents all the facts to its people.

For example, in an article in *Awake!*, Nicholas Kip, a Jehovah's Witness who teaches Greek at the high school level, gave the following testimony of his experience prior to becoming a Witness:

> I noticed that these [trinitarian] tract writers frequently manipulate the evidence, misrepresent it. On the other hand, the Society was quite honest in looking at all the evidence, all the possibilities, offering their conclusions, but then telling you to decide.[1]

At the end of his article is a brief appendix entitled "Some Comments by Greek Scholars on *The New World Translation of the Christian Greek Scriptures.*"[2] We shall here examine these comments to see what support they actually give to the Society's claim that their translation is scholastically sound. We shall also examine other attempts by the Watchtower Society to claim scholarly sanction for the NWT. And we shall compare these comments to some of the more notable scholarly reviews of the NWT published in major scholarly journals.

Edgar Goodspeed: "A Vast Array of Sound Serious Learning"?

Edgar J. Goodspeed was without question one of America's finest Greek scholars. So if Goodspeed endorsed the NWT, this fact is definitely worth noting and considering.

This endorsement is found in a letter from Goodspeed to Arthur Goux, a Jehovah's Witness worker at Bethel (the Society's headquarters in Brooklyn), dated December 8, 1950. Usually, as in the *Awake!* article, only a portion of the letter is cited. However, a copy of the letter in its entirety has been made available from the Society. A copy of this letter (see photocopy on the next page) was sent with a cover letter from the Watchtower Bible and Tract Society of New York, dated November 28, 1984, to Jim Kieferdorf of Dallas, Texas, who sent a copy to me. In their cover letter the Society stated that they were "enclosing a photocopy of a letter that Dr. Goodspeed wrote to Arthur Goux on December 8, 1950. . . ." In this letter, Goodspeed allegedly stated that he was "much pleased with the free, frank, and vigorous translation," and that, "it exhibits a vast array of sound serious learning, as I can testify."

Dr. Goodspeed has since died, so we cannot question him about the matter. However, there are some reasons to doubt the authenticity of the letter. The most important reason for doubting its authenticity is that it does not bear a written signature. Instead, where the signature should have appeared we find typed in the same typescript as the rest of the letter the words, "[signed] Edgar J. Goodspeed." Because there is no room for a signature, if

[c o p y]

VEGA VISTA

561 Perugia Way

BEL-AIR, LOS ANGELES 24

December 8, 1950

Dear Mr. Goux   *(incl NW Trans)*

Thank you very much for your books, which I am very glad to
see and have.   I am interested in the mission work of your
people, and its world wide scope, and much pleased with the free,
frank and vigorous translation.   It exhibits a vast array of
sound serious learning, as I can testify.   A few points of
difference of course strike an old translator, like me.   I am
sorry about your accent on Philippi, which is certainly wrong,
contrary to the well known classical rule, prevalent in English,
for all Greek and Latin proper names -- "Accent a long penult."
Even Shakespear's pronunciation shows it is Philip'pi.
(Pp 407, 578, etc.)

Strange such good scholars as your people evidently are
should not have noticed that apate Mt. 13:22 etc., is now known
to mean "pleasure."   And amphoteroi it is now well known means
both not only of two, but of five, six or seven, -- that is, as
we would say, "All," Acts 19:16.   There are many more present
imperatives in 1 Peter Chap. 1 than your people have perceived.
But I have thrashed these pts. all out in my New Testament
Translation problems, of course, long ago.

Again my renewed thanks.

Ever yours

[signed] Edgar J. Goodspeed

ever there was one, and because Goodspeed's name is typed in the same type as the rest of the letter, this makes it almost certain that this typed version of the letter is not the original (if there was an original). If Goodspeed did type and sign this letter, he must have signed it below the words "Ever yours"; yet he could not have done so, because there is no room for a signature below those words. It may be supposed that the words, "[signed] Edgar J. Goodspeed," were added afterward because the signature was too faint to be seen on a copy; but this is disproved by the fact that those words are typed in the same typescript as the rest of the letter. Therefore, we can deduce that this typed "copy" of the letter is not a copy of an original letter by Goodspeed. That being the case, it cannot constitute evidence that Goodspeed actually wrote such a letter. It is therefore up to the Society to produce the original, if one exists, from their files and explain why this doctored version has been disseminated in the past.

Second, it appears that this letter was not cited in any Watchtower publication in defense of the NWT until the 1980s. The first reference to this letter that I know of was in the *Watchtower* of March 15, 1982. Now, if it is true that the letter was not cited in the Society's publications until the 1980s, and yet the letter was written in 1950, it is very strange indeed that the Society did not bring this evidence to light earlier.

It is interesting to note that the Watchtower did claim in the early 1950s that Goodspeed had endorsed the NWT, but in a different context and using different words than the alleged 1950 letter by Goodspeed. In the *Watchtower* of September 1, 1952, an undated letter from an unnamed Witness addressed to a Mr. Lloyd D. Mattson is quoted at length. In this letter the unnamed Witness is quoted as commenting with reference to the NWT that "Goodspeed termed [it] 'an interesting and scholarly work.'"[3] This alleged statement of Goodspeed is not said to have been made in a letter; in fact, we are told nothing about when, where, why, or to whom Goodspeed made this statement. We are not even given Goodspeed's complete sentence. Without the complete statement and some information about the context in which it was made, there is no reason to take this alleged endorsement seriously. Moreover, it is interesting that the Society has twice claimed Goodspeed's endorsement, and both times it has been open to question.

Third, the criticisms of the NWT offered in this letter are extremely picayune, so much so that it is hard to imagine that it was actually written by Goodspeed. There are four criticisms made: (1) The word *Philippi* has the accent on the wrong syllable; (2) *apatē* in Matthew 13:22 should be translated "pleasure"; (3) *amphōteroi* can mean "all" as well as "both"; (4) there are more imperatives in 1 Peter 1 than are reflected in the NWT. What makes it surprising that these minor points should have been noticed by Goodspeed (yet he mentions no major points) is that the letter was allegedly written in December 1950. According to the Watchtower Society publications, the first volume of the NWT was released in August 1950, only four months prior to Goodspeed's letter. Moreover, even if we were to suppose (as the Witnesses will of course want to maintain) that there are no significant errors in the NWT, it is surely reasonable to suppose that Goodspeed, who was after all a trinitarian Christian, would have objected to some of their renderings of the key texts in the New Testament concerning the person of Christ. This lack of serious criticism also raises doubt as to the authenticity of the letter.

Finally, the testimony of others who talked with Goodspeed in the 1950s is that he did not esteem the NWT as highly as this letter suggests. Bill Cetnar, a former Witness who is now an evangelical Christian, was a worker at Bethel in the 1950s and was sent by the Society to interview Goodspeed and solicit an endorsement of the first volume of the Hebrew Scriptures (Old Testament) portion of the NWT. Cetnar writes:

> As I left, Dr. Goodspeed was asked if he would recommend the translation for the general public. He answered, "No, I'm afraid I couldn't do that. The grammar is regrettable. Be careful on the grammar. Be sure you have that right."[4]

Another testimony comes from the late Dr. Walter Martin, who met with Goodspeed in his home in Los Angeles in 1958 and talked with him for hours. According to Martin, Goodspeed forthrightly criticized the NWT rendering of John 1:1 and other texts.

Here are, then, four solid reasons to question the authenticity of the Goodspeed letter cited by the Watchtower Society in defense of the NWT: (1) The typed copy which the Society has sent out as documentation was certainly not typed by Goodspeed; (2) the Society did not begin citing the letter in defense of the NWT until the 1980s, some thirty years after the letter was supposedly written; (3) the criticisms of the NWT in the letter are so minor that it can hardly be supposed that an orthodox Christian, such as was Goodspeed, could have written it; and (4) other persons who interviewed Goodspeed years after he supposedly wrote the letter report that he was very critical of the NWT.

Having said all that, it must be added that it is still *possible* that Goodspeed did indeed write the letter. However, the alleged copy and the citations in the Society's publications do not constitute evidence that he did. Therefore, if the Jehovah's Witnesses wish to claim that Goodspeed endorsed their translation, they are going to have to come up with an original letter with Goodspeed's own signature as proof. Of course, they can continue to quote the alleged letter without properly verifying its authenticity, and they will probably convince themselves and many others who do not critically analyze the matter that Goodspeed did endorse the NWT. However, to anyone who wants the whole story and is not willing simply to take the Society's word for it, the mere citation of a letter of questionable authenticity proves nothing.

Alexander Thomson: "Skilled and Clever Scholars"?

The "scholarly review" which appears to be most often cited by the Jehovah's Witnesses in defense of the NWT was an article by an Alexander Thomson in a periodical called *The Differentiator* (April 1952), in which he wrote:

> The translation is evidently the work of skilled and clever scholars, who have sought to bring out as much of the true sense of the Greek text as the English language is capable of expressing.[5]

The Watchtower Society hails Thomson as a "Hebrew and Greek scholar." However, this seems to be an overstatement (to put it mildly). Thomson may have been versed in Hebrew and Greek to some extent, but so far as anyone has been able to determine he was not a scholar of these languages in any sense. That is, he appears not to have had any formal credentials; not to have taught the languages in an academic setting; and not to have written anything of a scholarly nature dealing with the languages. According to Bill Cetnar, Thomson denied the deity of Christ and was a "Universal Restitutionist," that is, he believed all men would eventually be saved.[6] Moreover, *The Differentiator* appears to have been a privately published journal without any scholarly reputation at all. It was published in the 1950s in Inglewood, California, and edited by Dr. F. N. Pohoriak (who by the mid-1980s was an invalid and could not discuss the matter).

In a later article in *The Differentiator*, Thomson wrote:

> On the whole the version was quite a good one, even though it was padded with many English words which had no equivalent in the Greek or Hebrew.[7]

This is an observation with which the Jehovah's Witnesses obviously cannot agree, and which they do not mention to their readers. Once again, therefore, the Jehovah's Witnesses are not giving us the whole story. Thomson's opinion is worth noting, of course, but it carries little weight, and it is not so positive as the Witnesses would like to think.

Robert McCoy: "Qualified Scholars"?

Robert M. McCoy wrote an article entitled "Jehovah's Witnesses and Their New Testament" for the *Andover Newton Quarterly* (Jan. 1963). In this article he stated:

> The translation of the New Testament is evidence of the presence in the movement of scholars qualified to deal intelligently with the many problems of Biblical translation.[8]

Who is Robert McCoy? According to a footnote in the article, "Mr. McCoy graduated with a B.D. [Bachelor of Divinity] in 1955 from the Boston University of Theology and with an S.T.M. [Sacred Theology Master] in 1962 from Andover Newton."[9] Although McCoy was fairly well educated, then, he does not have the credentials of a biblical scholar, nor is he recognized as one by other such scholars. Still, his opinion is interesting and worth hearing.

It should come as no surprise by now that McCoy had some less-than-flattering things to say about the NWT which the Society has not seen fit to pass on to its readers. One interesting comment concerned Matthew 5:9, which the NWT mistranslates "Happy are the peaceable" instead of "the peacemakers." McCoy notes, "One could question why the translators have not stayed closer to the literal meaning, as do most translators."[10] The answer, as those familiar with the Witnesses' teaching will know, is simple: The Jehovah's Witnesses do not believe that Christians should actively seek to bring about peace in the world, but rather should sit back passively and "peaceably" wait for the inevitable "end of this system of things."

Another comment by McCoy is the following: "In not a few instances the New World Translation contains passages which must be considered as 'theological translations.' This fact is particularly evident in those passages which express or imply the deity of Jesus Christ."[11] The term *theological translation* is borrowed from William A. Irwin, whom McCoy quotes as stating, "A 'theological translation' is no translation at all but merely a dogmatic perversion of the Bible."[12] This is hardly the sort of statement that can be construed as an endorsement of the translation.

In short, McCoy evidently regarded the NWT as the product of "scholars qualified to deal intelligently with the many problems of Biblical translations," but who frequently resorted to "theological translations," that is, "dogmatic perversions of the Bible," where the Bible disagrees with their theology. This is at best, then, a mixed review. Undoubtedly the Society would not cite the review if they knew that their readers would learn of McCoy's negative (and sound) criticisms of the NWT.

MacLean Gilmour: "An Unusual Competence in Greek"?

Another article from the *Andover Newton Quarterly* cited by the March 22, 1987, issue of *Awake!* was by S. MacLean Gilmour, who is quoted as having written, "The New Testament translation was made by a committee whose membership has never been revealed—a committee that possessed an unusual competence in Greek." The article was entitled "The Use and Abuse of the Book of Revelation," and was published in September 1966. A more complete excerpt of Gilmour's comments follows:

In 1950 the Jehovah's Witnesses published their *New World Translation of the New Testament*, and the preparation of the New World Old Testament translation is now far advanced. The New Testament translation was made by a committee whose membership has never been revealed—a committee that possessed an unusual competence in Greek and that made the Westcott and Hort Greek text basic to their translation. It is clear that doctrinal considerations influenced many turns of phrase, but the work is no crack-pot or pseudo-historical fraud.[13]

According to a footnote, "Dr. Gilmour is Norris Professor of New Testament at Andover Newton [Theological School] and editor of the school's *Quarterly*."[14] Gilmour's credentials as a scholar are not in question here; what is in question is whether he brought any scholarly knowledge or analysis to the matter of the NWT. Ian Croft of Concerned Christian Growth Ministries in Western Australia has made some excellent observations concerning Gilmour's unscholarly treatment of the NWT. First, he points out that the New Testament portion of the NWT is called the *New World Translation of the Christian Greek Scriptures*, not the *New World Translation of the New Testament*. Second, he notes that in this 1966 article Gilmour refers to the Old Testament portion of the NWT as "now far advanced," although it had been completed by 1960. Third, he observes that Gilmour does not actually discuss any specifics of the translation or even refer to it in his bibliography; instead he merely drops a reference to McCoy's article (discussed above). Croft rightly concludes that Gilmour's article "gives no evidence that he has read" the NWT or "even seen a copy" of it, and that his positive statement about the NWT "is based on the review done by another man."[15] Therefore, Gilmour's statement can hardly be construed as a scholarly endorsement of the NWT.

Thomas Winter: "Consistently Accurate"?

For several years the Watchtower Society has cited a favorable review in *The Classical Journal* of *The Kingdom Interlinear Translation of the Greek Scriptures*, a Greek-English interlinear of the New Testament portion of the NWT. This book review was written by Thomas N. Winter, a professor of Classics at the University of Nebraska. In it Winter praises the interlinear and states that "the translation by the anonymous committee is thoroughly up-to-date and consistently accurate."[16] What shall we make of this glowing appraisal?

On the positive side, it must be admitted that *The Classical Journal* is a reputable scholarly periodical (unlike *The Differentiator*), and that Winter is a bona fide scholar of the classical languages (i.e., Latin and Greek). Furthermore, in this case the Society is not quoting Winter out of context. Winter does indeed praise the *Kingdom Interlinear* to the skies, and does commend the translation itself; he has nothing negative to say about either the interlinear or the translation. Nor can he be dismissed as theologically biased in favor of the NWT or the Jehovah's Witnesses. In a letter dated October 3, 1980, to Kurt Goedelman of Personal Freedom Outreach, Winter makes the following comments:

> Many students of first Year Classical Greek are there with or because of a strong interest in the New Testament. My only purpose was to serve notice to the other Classics Professors that there was something available which might augment the motivation or enthusiasm of this portion of their students. As you may well imagine, I am not happy with the use now being made of the review, ten years, incidentally, since the time I wrote it—six years after it appeared.

Winter's review, therefore, is to some extent a scholarly endorsement of the NWT. However, this fact (which it must be remembered does not prove the NWT to be reliable) must be seen in its proper context. Winter is indeed a classics scholar, and is therefore competent in classical Greek. But is he competent as a scholar in biblical Greek? The Greek used in the Christian Greek Scriptures was *koine* ("common") Greek, not classical Greek. That the differences between these two varieties of Greek could be significant for the meaning of the text is confirmed by the Watchtower Society, which states in its Bible dictionary article on Greek:

> Since the writers of the inspired Christian Scriptures were concerned with getting their message across with understanding to all the people, it was not the classical, but the *koine* Greek that they used. . . . *Koine* was a development from the classical Attic Greek. While Attic Greek contained many vernacular expressions, the *Koine* added a great many more, making it more cosmopolitan, simplifying the grammar, and so forth.[17]

In pointing out the differences between classical and *koine* Greek, we are not denying that Prof. Winter is aware of the differences, or even that he is able to read with understanding Greek of different periods and styles. However, there is some significant evidence indicating that Winter is less familiar with biblical Greek scholarship than he is with classical Greek and Latin scholarship.

Specifically, it is instructive to note what feature of the interlinear portion of the *Kingdom Interlinear* Winter found so unusual and helpful that he would say of it, "This is no ordinary interlinear." That feature is the fact that under each Greek word is a single English word, spaced so that the meaning of the Greek words can be seen immediately. This enables the student to read through the Greek text with more understanding than if the regular English translation appeared uninterrupted under the Greek text, especially since Greek word order often differs from English word order.[18]

Now, while this particular feature of the *Kingdom Interlinear* is commendable, it is hardly unique. For instance, Zondervan Publishing House publishes a Greek-English interlinear of the New Testament, written by Alfred Marshall, which incorporates the same feature.[19] It is interesting to note, then, that Winter does not compare the *Kingdom Interlinear* to Marshall's interlinear or some other interlinear of the New Testament. Instead, he compares the *Kingdom Interlinear* to "an ordinary interlinear," the Hart and Osborn interlinear of the Latin poet *Vergil*. This fact suggests that Winter may not be as familiar with Greek New Testament reference works as one would prefer for a reviewer of a Greek-English New Testament interlinear.

Still, Winter is quite correct in saying that the interlinear portion of the *Kingdom Interlinear* is well done. It uses the Westcott-Hort Greek text, and underneath is a literal word-for-word rendering of each Greek word, produced by the Watchtower Society. This word-for-word rendering is generally accurate, although not quite always. Indeed, many of the errors in the NWT can be seen easily by comparing it with the *Kingdom Interlinear!*

It is Winter's recommendation of the translation itself that is of concern here. As has already been pointed out, Winter is more of a classicist than a biblical scholar. The one example he gives to illustrate the "consistently accurate" quality of the NWT is a case in point. "Where both the *King James* and the *Revised Standard*, for instance, have 'wise men' for the Greek *magos* (e.g.,*Matt.* 2:1, 2:7, 2:16), the *Kingdom Interlinear* has 'astrologers,' a more correct and informative rendition."[20] Although it is true that the Magi were studied in astrology, saying they were "astrologers" gives the totally misleading impression that they were religious crackpots who wrote horoscope columns for the *Babylon Times*. The fact is that the Magi were a monotheistic priesthood of the Zoroastrian religion trained in the philosophical, religious, and political wisdom of their people. While for the most part the religious practices of the Magi as a class were roughly synonymous with occultic "magic" (which derives from the word *Magi*), it is evident that the Magi were much more than astrologers or even occultists.[21] It is therefore best to leave the word untranslated, or use some general translation such as "wise men," as the King James Version and the Revised Standard Version have done. Ironically, then, Winter's single example of the translation of the NWT is an example of the shallowness of its scholarship.

In conclusion, Winter's article is the closest thing to a genuine endorsement by a Greek scholar, but his apparent lack of familiarity with biblical scholarship and the superficial treatment he gives the NWT itself indicate that his comments fall short of a competent scholarly evaluation of the NWT.

Eerdmans': One of the "Main 20th-Century English Translations"?

The *Eerdmans' Handbook to the Bible* is one of the most reliable and useful of all the many Bible handbooks that are currently in print. Soundly evangelical, it is a standard reference work for Christians who are non-professional but serious students of the Bible.

It may come as a surprise to learn that the Watchtower Society has cited this handbook as making a favorable comment on the NWT. The March 15, 1982, *Watchtower* noted that this handbook "lists the *New World Translation* among the 14 'main 20th-century English translations'" (p. 19). The questions that come immediately to mind are, in what sense is this meant, and does the handbook say anything else about the NWT?

A quick look at the handbook makes it immediately apparent that by "main" translations the handbook means translations receiving wide circulation and use, not the best or most accurate ones. This fact is confirmed by the comment next to the listing of the NWT: "Produced by the Jehovah's Witnesses, emphasizing their interpretation of particular texts."[22] This is a rather colorless and evenhanded way of saying that the translation is biased in favor of the Jehovah's Witnesses' doctrine.

By no means, then, can the listing of the NWT in the *Eerdmans' Handbook to the Bible* be legitimately construed as an endorsement or recognition of scholarly accuracy.

Colwell: "The Best New Testament"?

In a "Questions from Readers" column in *The Watchtower* (Jan. 1, 1963), the Society cited a book by E. C. Colwell titled *What Is the Best New Testament?* as implicitly demonstrating the accuracy of the NWT:

> This book is published by the Chicago University Press and was first printed in 1952. In 1947 Professor Colwell made a study of a number of translations and put them to the test as to sixty-four citations in the book of John. The book contains what Professor Colwell considers the correct rendering of each of those sixty-four citations. The New World Translation was not released until 1950, hence Professor Colwell could not include this translation in his list of tested ones.
>
> However, if anyone will look up what Professor Colwell has to say about these sixty-four citations and will compare these with the New World Translation he will see that the New World Translation merits a score of sixty-four along with Dr. Goodspeed's translation of the Christian Greek Scriptures, which the book gives a perfect score of sixty-four.[23]

This argument in defense of the NWT has been repeated by the Jehovah's Witnesses many times, even circulated on single sheets of paper with the information somewhat garbled (e.g., Colwell's name spelled Caldwell). It is evidently a popular argument.

There is no question here about Colwell's credentials. Ernest Cadman Colwell is a famous Greek scholar, roughly of the same stature as Good-

speed. The problem here is that Colwell's book has been greatly mis-
construed. The key chapter of the book is chapter 9, "How Accurate Is
Your New Testament?" Colwell begins the chapter with this paragraph:

> If you care about your New Testament, you will want to know what "make" it is,
> who translated it, and, above all, how accurate it is. The translator may dimin-
> ish, but he cannot materially increase, the accuracy of the particular Greek
> New Testament from which he makes his translation. In the matter of accuracy,
> therefore, the primary question is, "How accurate a New Testament was it
> translated from?"[24]

As an aside, we may note Colwell's statement that if we care about our
New Testament we will want to know "who translated it," something the
Watchtower Society is unwilling to let its people know (although the main
members of the NWT translation committee *are* known[25]). Next, we should
notice Colwell's important observation that a translator "may diminish, but
he cannot materially increase, the accuracy of the particular Greek New
Testament from which he makes his translation." What this means is that
a translation cannot be any more accurate than the Greek text on which it
is based, no matter how good a job the translator does; but it can be far
less accurate if the translator does not do his job correctly. The point here
as it relates to the NWT is that scholars are not critical of the NWT for the
Greek text on which it is based, namely, the Westcott-Hort text, but for the
way in which that text has been translated into English. Colwell makes his
concern explicit when he says that *his* question is, "How accurate a New
Testament was it translated from?" Thus, he does not address the matter of
how good a job the translators did rendering the Greek into English, but
rather, of the accuracy of the Greek text they chose on which to base their
translation.

Colwell then goes on to list seventeen translations "roughly in the order
of their accuracy," with Goodspeed listed first and the King James Version
listed at the bottom. He then continues as follows:

> The ranking of these translations was based originally on the translator's
> own statements as to their source; but this has been checked and corrected by
> a test as to the relationship of each of these translations to two forms of the
> Greek New Testament—the Westcott and Hort text and the Textus Receptus or
> Received Text. I carried out this test for the entire content of the Gospel of
> John. In this gospel the two Greek texts were compared verse by verse; and,
> from the large list of differences noted, sixty-four passages were selected in
> which even the freest English translation must show which of the two Greek
> texts it supports.[26]

Colwell goes on to explain that the Westcott-Hort text was regarded
as the best text, and the Textus Receptus as the worst. This means that
any translation based solely on the Textus Receptus would automatically

receive a score of zero, while any translation based solely on the Westcott-Hort text would be assured of receiving a perfect score of sixty-four. Colwell even states that he restricted his test to passages where the textual basis of the translation would be apparent even in "the freest English translation." In other words, no matter how loosely the translation paraphrases the text, and, we would add, no matter how inaccurate the translation itself is, the differences in these particular sixty-four texts on which the test focused were designed to screen out such matters and reveal only which Greek text was used.

It is true, therefore, that on the basis of Colwell's test the NWT rates a "perfect score" of sixty-four, because in the sixty-four verses that Colwell chose the NWT follows the Westcott-Hort text. But this fact only proves that on the basis of Colwell's test we may say that the NWT translators used the best Greek text as the basis of their translation, not that the translation itself was accurate in its rendition of the Greek text into English.

Another thing to keep in mind is that no one claims that the NWT is a bad translation all the way through. Rather, the usual claim is that the translation is biased in a large number of theologically critical passages, that the arguments in defense of the NWT renderings of those critical passages are for the most part without scholarly support, and that as a whole the translation is uneven and lacking in professional scholarly quality.

Once again, therefore, the Watchtower Society has not told the whole story in its citation of Colwell's test in defense of the NWT.

Some Comments by Top Scholars

In contrast to the various citations discussed above, some out of context, some by unqualified persons, there have been a few biblical scholars of unquestioned credentials who have strongly criticized the NWT. We shall mention just two, one on the Christian Greek Scriptures and the other on the Hebrew Scriptures.

Bruce M. Metzger is a biblical Greek scholar of the highest order. A professor of New Testament Greek at Princeton Theological Seminary, he was a co-editor of the United Bible Societies' *Greek New Testament* and the author of the UBS *Textual Commentary on the New Testament* (1975), among many other scholarly works. He has written three articles on the Jehovah's Witnesses and the NWT in which he argues that "the Jehovah's Witnesses have incorporated in their translation of the New Testament several quite erroneous renderings of the Greek."[27] Metzger backs up this charge with analyses of the NWT rendering of John 1:1 and other texts.

H. H. Rowley was an Old Testament Hebrew scholar at the University of Manchester in England, a school renowned for its biblical scholars (e.g., S. G. F. Brandon, F. F. Bruce), and the author of scholarly books on the Old Testament. He wrote two reviews of the Hebrew Scriptures portion of

the NWT, the first of which reviewed the Genesis-Ruth volume and was entitled, "How Not to Translate the Bible":

> The translators have their own views on Hebrew tenses, but prefer to offer
> them to uninstructed readers before submitting their justification of them to
> the scrutiny of scholars. This is probably wise. [That is, scholars would never
> agree with the translators' views on Hebrew tenses.] They profess to offer a
> rendering into modern English which is as faithful as possible. In fact, the
> jargon which they use is often scarcely English at all, and it reminds one of
> nothing so much as a schoolboy's first painful beginnings in translating Latin
> into English. The translation is marked by a wooden literalism which will only
> exasperate any intelligent reader—if such it finds—and instead of showing
> the reverence for the Bible which the translators profess, it is an insult to
> the Word of God.[28]

After giving four examples from the first half of Genesis alone, Rowley
states: "Even readers who know only English will wonder whether writers
who are so poorly equipped to write their own language can really be
authorities on Hebrew tenses!"

Following several more examples from the early chapters of Genesis,
Rowley concludes:

> From beginning to end this volume is a shining example of how the Bible should
> not be translated, and a reminder that the Bible is great literature, which
> deserves to be translated by those who have a feeling for style and who both
> understand the original and know how to express its meaning with elegance.[29]

The second review was of the volume containing 1 Samuel to Esther.
Rowley has this to say:

> The review of the first volume involved the reviewer in a long correspondence
> with Brooklyn, not very fruitful in its results but warmly friendly in character—
> despite one acknowledgment of his "frank but faithless" letter—so that he now
> feels something of the reluctance with which one criticises friends when he says
> that the second volume shows the same faults as the first. There is the same
> wooden literalness and inelegance that marked the earlier volume, giving to the
> rendering something of the harshness that Aquila's Greek version had. . . . In
> some cases inelegance is combined with obscurity. . . . In general the transla-
> tors show that they understand the Hebrew, even though they cannot express
> its meaning in elegant English, but occasionally their knowledge is defective.[30]

Evaluating Alleged Scholarly Endorsements

It is likely that in the future the Jehovah's Witnesses will cite additional
sources as giving some kind of endorsement of the NWT. In conclusion, then,
it will be helpful to set forth basic principles to evaluate such statements.

1. *Is complete and verifiable documentation available?* Typically, the Watchtower publications in which these endorsements are cited do not give complete bibliographical details. Seek a photocopy of the original document *in its entirety* whenever possible before attempting to evaluate the statement. If there is any substantial reason to doubt the authenticity of the quotation (as is the case with the citation of Goodspeed), refuse to accept it as evidence until documentation is found.

2. *Is the author a scholar in the field?* I employ a threefold test to determine if a person is a scholar in any field: (a) Does he or she hold a doctorate or other postgraduate degree in the field? (b) Does he or she hold a teaching position in the field at an accredited school on the undergraduate or graduate level? (c) Has he or she written significant articles or books in the field that have been published by reputable scholarly periodicals or publishing houses? If the answer to any one of these three questions (*not* necessarily all three) is yes, then the person is a scholar in that field; if not, then I hold that he or she is not a scholar in that field. If a person writing a review or commenting on the NWT (or any other translation) does not meet one of the above criteria of scholarship, then in my opinion the evaluation of the NWT cannot be considered "scholarly"—whether or not it is accurate. Note that nonscholars can be right; the point is that the Society cannot legitimately quote totally unknown individuals with no academic credentials or scholarly position as scholars in support of their translation.

3. *Has the person brought biblical or linguistic scholarship to bear on the evaluation?* Even if a top-drawer biblical Greek scholar were to commend the NWT, I would want to see some evidence that he or she had brought scholarly expertise to bear in evaluating the NWT. At the very least I would want to see some evidence that the scholar had actually obtained a copy of the NWT and studied it firsthand. So, for instance, if a Greek scholar commends the NWT but does not even get the title right and makes no specific comments on the accuracy of the translation, that opinion does not deserve to be called scholarly.

4. *Has the scholar been quoted in context?* Sometimes the problem is not at all with the scholarship of the person being quoted, but rather with the Society quoting the scholar out of context. In such cases, reading the original in its entirety is the only way to get the whole story.

Asking questions like these is necessary if the alleged endorsements of the NWT are to be correctly analyzed and evaluated.

Appendix **B**

Word Study:
Cross or Stake?

S ome insights into how Jehovah's Witnesses improperly interpret biblical words have already been gained from our study of their teaching on the divine name (chapter 8). Here, though, I shall examine the
Witnesses' handling of the Greek word *stauros*, translated "torture stake"
in the NWT and "cross" by virtually all other translators. This is a more traditional kind of word study, and one which well illustrates the way Witnesses frequently mistranslate and misinterpret key words in the Bible.

The Perils of Word Studies

The study of individual words in the Bible can be extremely fruitful. At the
same time, however, a number of serious mistakes can be made in interpreting isolated words. In recent years a number of excellent books by evangelical scholars have appeared pointing out the sorts of mistakes in this
area that are often made both by heretical groups and orthodox Christians.[1]
The fact is that heretics are not the only ones who make mistakes in
their word studies in the Bible. Christians, though their beliefs on the essential, life-and-death matters revealed in Scripture are faithful to Scripture,

141

are not perfect in their interpretations of the Bible. We have made mistakes in the past, and we make mistakes today, and we frankly admit it, as the above-mentioned evangelical publications attest (see note 1). I say this here, lest anyone suppose my claim is that evangelical Christians conduct flawless word studies while Jehovah's Witnesses constantly botch theirs. Rather, what I seek to show in this appendix is that Jehovah's Witnesses employ faulty methods of word studies to introduce new teachings which contradict the Bible.

It is important to note here that we are not engaged in "fighting over words" in the unprofitable sense about which the apostle Paul warned us (2 Tim. 2:14). Jehovah's Witnesses, challenged on their mishandling of key biblical words such as *stauros* ("cross"), have often retreated behind a pious refusal to fight over words. Yet it is they who have challenged the historic Christian faith and condemned it as apostate on the basis of their novel interpretations of such words. What Paul discouraged was pointless arguing over words where no substance was at issue. (A modern violation of Paul's command would be, for instance, if Christians were to argue over whether to call their gathering a church, assembly, or congregation; the words are synonymous, and such a debate would be pointless.) In the very next sentence Paul commands Timothy to be careful to interpret Scripture correctly (2:15).

What, then, are some of the common mistakes that can be made in biblical word studies? I commented on this question briefly in chapter 1, but there is more to be said. One mistake that crops up again and again is the assumption that the original or earliest meaning of a word must be its "true" meaning. That this is not so can be seen from the example of the history of the word *nice:* In Old English the word first means "foolish," and only more recently comes to mean "pleasant."[2]

Another mistake is to insist that the true meaning of a word must be some basic meaning common to all of its uses. For instance, in the word *bar* one can discern amidst most or all of its diverse uses the common notion of a straight hard object; yet no one fluent in English would suppose that the bar which controls who may become lawyers needs or uses a physical "bar" of any sort.[3]

Third, it is sometimes mistakenly assumed that, because a word can be used with different meanings, any or all of those meanings can apply whenever the word is used. To offer a ridiculous example, the word *pitcher* in the sentence "The pitcher threw the ball" simply cannot mean a container designed to hold a beverage. Or, to give a biblical example, although the word *angelos* can mean either a human "messenger" or an "angel" in the sense of a spirit sent from God, in Luke 7:24 the word must be translated "messengers," since they are said to be sent by John the Baptist.

Though more types of word study errors could be mentioned, these are sufficient for our purposes. The rest of this appendix will examine the manner in which the Jehovah's Witnesses have misinterpreted the Greek word *stauros.*

Stauros

Nicholas Kip is one of the very few Jehovah's Witnesses who can claim to have known Greek before becoming a Witness. In his testimony article in *Awake!* magazine in 1987, Kip wrote:

> Suzanne would come to me [before his conversion to the Witnesses, while she was studying with them] and ask:
> "Oh, Nicholas, here's a word that Karen and I studied in the Bible. Could *stauros* just mean 'stake'?"
> "Well, sure. It does mean 'stake.' I don't know how they ever got 'cross' out of *stauros.* But I'm not surprised. The Christian church has been doing things like that at least since Constantine's time."[4]

It is highly doubtful that a professing Christian would make such a disparaging remark about what the church has been doing "since Constantine's time." This sounds as if Kip is projecting back into his pre-Witness days an attitude he acquired only later as a Jehovah's Witness.

To Nicholas Kip's comment, "I don't know how they ever got 'cross' out of *stauros,*" there is a fairly simple answer. Although the most basic meaning of *stauros* was of a straight stick or stake, it was commonly used in Jesus' time to refer to a variety of wooden instruments of execution used by the Romans, probably most often of the cross.

As has already been explained, words often have meanings that extend beyond their original etymology. Kip himself seems to recognize this point when later in his article he notes that words can have a variety of meanings.[5] Now, the fact is that the Greek word *stauros* was often used to refer to the Roman instrument of execution that was in Latin called the *crux,* from which (as the Watchtower itself has stated[6]) we derive the word *cross.* That is "how they . . . got 'cross' out of *stauros.*" In truth, the cross could and did take on a variety of shapes, notably those similar to the Greek letter *tau* (T) and the plus sign (+), occasionally using two diagonal beams (X), as well as (infrequently) a simple upright stake with no crosspiece. To argue that only the last-named form was used, or that *stauros* could be used only for that form, is contradictory to the actual historical facts and is based on a naive restriction of the term to its original or simplest meaning. Indeed, the words *stauros* and *crux* were sometimes used for the entire cross, at other times for the upright part alone, and at other times for the crosspiece alone. These historical facts about the *stauros* or *crux* have been discussed in great detail in reputable scholarly works, and there is really no doubt about them.[7]

Since the word *stauros* could refer to a cross, the upright part of a cross, the crossbeam, or to an upright stake with no crossbeam, there is no basis in the word itself for the Jehovah's Witnesses' contention that Jesus did not die on a cross. The question now is, does the Bible tell us anything else of relevance to this question? The answer is yes. In John 20:25 the apostle Thomas, in expressing his doubt concerning Jesus' resurrection, said, "Unless I see in his hands the print of *the nails* and stick my finger into the print of *the nails* . . ." (NWT). According to Thomas, then, more than one nail was used to impale Jesus' hands to the *stauros*. The most natural conclusion is that two nails were used, one for each hand, and that therefore the hands were separated on a crossbeam of some sort. (It might be helpful to keep in mind here that the word *nail* might better be rendered "spike," since we are not talking about a thin little nail.) Once this fact is noticed, the conclusion seems unavoidable that Jesus died on a cross.

At this point, most Jehovah's Witnesses will probably appeal to W. E. Vine's *Expository Dictionary of New Testament Words*, or to similar works, as Jehovah's Witnesses invariably do when this question comes up.[8] However, neither Vine nor any of the other authors who deny that Jesus died on a cross and are cited by the Watchtower publications, so far as I can tell, have dealt with the historical and archaeological evidence outlined above. Moreover, none of them appear to have dealt with the matter of John 20:25. Despite the fact that Vine's work is generally well respected among evangelical Christians, on this matter he is flat wrong.

Now, admittedly the shape of the *stauros* is of little consequence. But the Jehovah's Witnesses, by making such an issue of it, have staked (pun intended) their reputation as accurate interpreters of the Bible on a word study that any person acquainted with the literature on the subject should realize is shallow.

Notes

Introduction

1. See Norman L. Geisler (ed.), *Inerrancy* (Grand Rapids: Zondervan Publishing House, 1979), 493–502.

2. Edmond Charles Gruss, *Apostles of Denial: An Examination and Exposé of the History, Doctrines and Claims of the Jehovah's Witnesses* (Phillipsburg, N.J.: Presbyterian & Reformed Publishing Co., 1975).

3. Moises Silva, *Has the Church Misread the Bible? The History of Interpretation in the Light of Current Issues,* Foundations of Contemporary Interpretation, Vol. 1 (Grand Rapids: Zondervan Publishing House—Academie Books, 1987), iii.

Chapter 1 *Approaching the Bible in Dialogue*

1. *You Can Live Forever in Paradise on Earth* (Brooklyn: Watchtower Bible and Tract Society [hereafter WTBTS], 1982), 55.

2. Ibid., 188.

3. *Worldwide Security Under the "Prince of Peace"* (WTBTS, 1986), 10.

4. *United in Worship of the Only True God* (WTBTS, 1983), 24–26.

5. *The Kingdom Interlinear Translation of the Greek Scriptures* (WTBTS, 1985), 7 (hereafter *KIT* [1985]).

6. *New World Translation of the Holy Scriptures: With References* (WTBTS, 1984), 6 (hereafter *NWT* [1984]); *"All Scripture Is Inspired of God and Beneficial"* (WTBTS, 1963), 304–313.

7. *NWT* (1984), 6; *All Scripture,* 314–18.

8. In fact, the Witnesses appear to hold that Matthew himself translated his Gospel into Greek; *Insight on the Scriptures* (WTBTS, 1988), 2:353.

9. *NWT* (1984), 6.

10. *Reasoning from the Scriptures* (WTBTS, 1985), 63–64; *You Can Live Forever,* 52–53; *The Watchtower* (July 15, 1990):27–29.

145

11. See the appendices in the NWT (1984).

12. NWT (1984), 1585.

13. *You Can Live Forever*, 203–7.

14. *Insight on the Scriptures*, 2:1130.

15. *Reasoning*, 204.

16. "Five Common Fallacies—Don't Be Fooled by Them!" *Awake!* (May 22, 1990):12.

17. Ibid., 14.

18. Ibid., 12–13.

19. *Reasoning*, 7.

20. Ibid., 65.

21. "Five Common Fallacies," 13.

22. For an excellent discussion of the relation between logic, the Bible, and theology, see John M. Frame, *Doctrine of the Knowledge of God: A Theology of Lordship* (Grand Rapids: Baker Book House, 1987). The best textbook on logic written specifically for Christians is Norman L. Geisler and Ronald M. Brooks, *Come, Let Us Reason: An Introduction to Logical Thinking* (Grand Rapids: Baker Book House, 1990).

23. *United in Worship*, 26.

24. For a fairly technical treatment of this question by an evangelical writer, see Moises Silva, *Biblical Words and Their Meaning: An Introduction to Lexical Analysis* (Grand Rapids: Zondervan Publishing House, 1983).

25. *Reasoning from the Scriptures*, 205.

26. Ibid., 148–49.

27. See n. 15.

Chapter 2 *Evangelicals, Jehovah's Witnesses, and the Bible*

1. For a discussion of this question, see this author's book *Why You Should Believe in the Trinity: An Answer to Jehovah's Witnesses* (Grand Rapids: Baker Book House, 1989), 111–22.

2. For example, see the reference to Ralph Martin's comment on Philippians 2:6 in the Watchtower booklet *Should You Believe in the Trinity?* (WTBTS, 1989), 25; for a discussion of Martin's interpretation of the verse see this author's *Why You Should Believe in the Trinity*, 101–4.

Chapter 3 *The Watchtower: Biblical Servant or Unbiblical Master?*

1. See especially Duane Magnani, *Bible Students? Do Jehovah's Witnesses Really Study the Bible? An Analysis* (Clayton, Calif.: Witness Inc., 1983); Duane Magnani, *Who Is the Faithful and Wise Servant? A Study of Authority over Jehovah's Witnesses*, 4th ed. (Clayton, Calif.: Witness Inc., 1988). References to these books in this chapter are to pages where Watchtower literature is reproduced for reference purposes.

2. *The Watchtower* (Feb. 1, 1952):79, in Magnani, *Who*, 163.

3. *The Watchtower* (Feb. 15, 1981):19, in Magnani, *Bible Students?*, photo #50.

4. *1983 Yearbook of Jehovah's Witnesses* (WTBTS, 1982), 21, in Magnani, *Bible Students?*, photo #64.

5. *Qualified to Be Ministers* (WTBTS, 1967), 156, in Magnani, *Who*, 91.

6. *The Watchtower* (Sept. 15, 1964):574, in Magnani, *Bible Students?*, photo #5.

7. *The Watch Tower* (April 1, 1919):105, in Magnani, *Bible Students?*, photo #7.

8. *Informant* (Oct. 1943):2, in Magnani, *Bible Students?*, photo #1.

9. *The Watch Tower* (Mar. 1, 1923):68, in Magnani, *Who*, 111.

10. *United in Worship of the Only True God* (WTBTS, 1983), 24, in Magnani, *Bible Students?*, photo #12.

11. See n. 3.

12. *The Watchtower* (Aug. 15, 1950):263, in Magnani, *Bible Students?*, photo #52.

13. See n. 3.

14. *Reasoning from the Scriptures*, 136.

15. *The Watchtower* (Feb. 1, 1952): 79–80, in Magnani, *Who*, 163–64.

16. *The Watchtower* (April 1, 1972):197, in Magnani, *Who*, 78.

17. *1983 Yearbook of Jehovah's Witnesses*, in Duane Magnani and Arthur Barrett, *Dialogue with Jehovah's Witnesses*, Vol. 1 (Clayton, Calif.: Witness, Inc., 1983), i.

18. *Reasoning from the Scriptures*, 134, 136, 205.

19. See especially ibid., 134.

20. *The Watch Tower* (Sept. 15, 1910):298, in Magnani, *Bible Students?*, photo #82.

21. *The Watchtower* (Aug. 15, 1981):28–29, in Magnani, *Bible Students?*, photo #83.

22. *You Can Live Forever in Paradise on Earth* (WTBTS, 1982), 193, 195, in Magnani, *Who*, 94, 95.

23. *The Watchtower* (June 15, 1957):370; (Dec. 15, 1977):751; (Feb. 1, 1985):21; in Magnani, *Who*, 76, 84, 85.

24. *Insight on the Scriptures* (WTBTS, 1988), s.v. "Faithful and Discreet Slave," 1:806.

25. *Aid to Bible Understanding*, 839.

26. See n. 3.

Chapter 4 *The New World Translation*

1. *KIT* (1985), 5.

2. On these biblical texts, see this author's *Why You Should Believe in the Trinity: An Answer to Jehovah's Witnesses* (Grand Rapids: Baker Book House, 1989), 91–98, 104–8; and on John 1:1, see this author's *Jehovah's Witnesses, Jesus Christ, and the Gospel of John* (Grand Rapids: Baker Book House, 1989), Part One.

3. See n. 2.

Chapter 5 *The Foundation of Jehovah's Witness Beliefs*

1. For most of the information here see *Jehovah's Witnesses in the Divine Purpose* (WTBTS, 1959), 14–22, and M. James Penton, *Apocalypse Delayed: The Story of Jehovah's Witnesses* (Toronto: University of Toronto Press, 1985), 13–27.

2. Cited in *Jehovah's Witnesses in the Divine Purpose*, 14.

3. On the relation of Adventism to evangelicalism, see Kenneth R. Samples, "From Controversy to Crisis: An Updated Assessment of Seventh-day Adventism," *Christian Research Journal* 11, 1 (Summer 1988):8–14.

4. See Dean C. Halverson, "88 Reasons: What Went Wrong?" *Christian Research Journal* 11, 2 (Fall 1988):14–18.

5. *Reasoning from the Scriptures*, 424.

6. Ibid., 148–49.

7. This has been the usual view of the Jehovah's Witnesses, as in *Aid to Bible Understanding*, 665, 1542.

8. For a more complete documentation of and response to the Jehovah's Witnesses' views on this subject, see Duane Magnani, *The Heavenly Weather Man* (Clayton, Calif.: Witness Inc., 1987), 197–222.

9. *Insight on the Scriptures*, 1:1060–61.

10. See Hugh Ross, *The Fingerprint of God*, 2d. ed., (Orange, Calif.: Promise Publishers, 1991).

11. E.g., *Reasoning from the Scriptures*, 145.

Chapter 6 *The Jehovah's Witness Hermeneutical Circle*

1. For a survey of Christian views on war, see *War: Four Christian Views*, ed. Robert G. Clouse (Downers Grove, Ill.: InterVarsity Press, 1981). Two of the more thoughtful books by evangelicals on war in the modern context are Ronald J. Sider and Richard K. Taylor, *Nuclear Holocaust and Christian Hope: A Book for Christian Peacemakers* (Downers Grove, Ill.: InterVarsity Press, 1982), written from a basically pacifist perspective; and Keith B. Payne and Karl I. Payne, *A Just Defense: The Use of Force, Nuclear Weapons, and Our Conscience* (Portland, Ore.: Multnomah Press, 1987). I do not agree completely with either book, but recommend both to persons who want to understand the issues and not just have their own views reinforced.

2. In this book I have deliberately focused attention away from these more overt aspects of organizational control over the thinking of Jehovah's Witnesses and emphasized instead those factors which are more "normal" and from which evangelicals have something to learn. For literature focusing on the way the Watchtower organization controls the thinking of its followers, please contact Bethel Ministries, Comments from the Friends, or Witness Inc. (see "For Further Information" at the end of this book).

Chapter 7 *Case Study in Interpretation: Luke 23:43*

1. Joachim Jeremias, *New Testament Theology*, Vol. I: *The Proclamation of Jesus* (New York: Charles Scribner's Sons, 1971), 36.

2. NWT (1984), 1279 note.

3. Bruce M. Metzger, *A Textual Commentary on the Greek New Testament* (New York: United Bible Societies, 1971), 181–82.

4. NWT (1984), 1564–66.

5. *Insight on the Scriptures*, s.v. "Paradise," 2:575.

6. Ibid., 95–96; *"Let Your Kingdom Come"* (WTBTS, 1981), 127–38; *Reasoning from the Scriptures*, 95–96; *Insight on the Scriptures*, s.v. "Appointed Times of the Nations," 1:132–35.

7. *Insight*, ibid., 1:133–34.

8. Joachim Jeremias, *"Paradeisos,"* in *Theological Dictionary of the New Testament*, ed. Gerhard Friedrich, trans. Geoffrey W. Bromiley (Grand Rapids: William B. Eerdmans Publishing Co., 1967), 5:766–69.

9. Hans Bietenhard and Colin Brown, "Paradise," in *The New International Dictionary of New Testament Theology*, ed. Colin Brown (Grand Rapids: William B. Eerdmans Publishing Co., 1976), 2:761, cited in *Reasoning from the Scriptures*, 286.

10. Bietenhard and Brown, "Paradise," 2:761.

11. James Hastings, "Paradise," in *Dictionary of the Bible*, ed. James Hastings (New York: Scribner's Sons, 1909), 3:669–70, cited in *Aid to Bible Understanding*, 1269; *Reasoning from the Scriptures*, 286; and *Insight*, s.v. "Paradise," 2:575–76.

12. Hastings, "Paradise," 3:671.

13. Robert M. Bowman, Jr., "The Whitewashing of the Watchtower: How Jehovah's Witnesses Are Defending Thefir Faith," *Forward* 9, 1 (Spring/Summer 1986): 9–14; *Jehovah's Witnesses, Jesus Christ, and the Gospel of John* (Grand Rapids: Baker Book House, 1989).

14. *Insight*, s.v. "Paradise," 2:576.

15. Jeremias, *New Testament Theology*, 768.

16. See n. 14.

17. *Revelation—Its Grand Climax at Hand!* (WTBTS, 1988); see David A. Reed's review in *Christian Research Journal* 11, 3 (Summer 1989).

18. *You Can Live Forever*, 171; see also *Reasoning from the Scriptures*, 287.

19. *Insight*, ibid., 2:575.

20. *Reasoning from the Scriptures*, 423–24.

21. Jeremias, "Paradise," 768.

22. On the relation of Paradise to heaven see Herbert Lockyer, *Death and the Life Hereafter* (Grand Rapids: Baker Book House, 1975), 94–99.

Chapter 8 *Jehovah's Witnesses and the Divine Name*

1. *The Divine Name That Will Endure Forever* (WTBTS, 1984), 8.

2. Ibid., 9–10.

3. Ibid., 6.

4. Charles R. Gianotti, "The Meaning of the Divine Name YHWH," *Bibliotheca Sacra* 142 (Jan.-Mar. 1985):38–51.

5. On Exodus 3:14, especially as it relates to John 8:58, see Robert M. Bowman, Jr., *Jehovah's Witnesses, Jesus Christ, and the Gospel of John* (Grand Rapids: Baker Book House, 1989), 121–29.

6. *Insight*, s.v. "Jehovah," 2:8.

7. Albert Pietersma, "Kyrios or Tetragram: A Renewed Quest for the Original LXX," in *De Septuaginta: Studies in Honour of John William Wevers on His Sixty-fifth Birthday*, ed. Albert Pietersma and Claude Cox (Mississauga, Ont.: Benben Publications, 1984), 86–87.

8. Ibid., 85–101; Robert H. Countess, *The Jehovah's Witnesses' New Testament: A Critical Analysis of the New World Translation of the Christian Greek Scriptures* (Phillipsburg, N.J.: Presbyterian & Reformed Publishing Co., 1982), 27–30; D. R. DeLacey, "'One Lord' in Pauline Christology," in *Christ the Lord: Studies in Christology Presented to Donald Guthrie*, ed. Harold H. Rowdon (Leicester, England: Inter-Varsity Press, 1982), 191–94; Doug Mason, *JEHOVAH in the Jehovah's Witnesses' New World Translation* (Manhattan Beach, Calif.: Bethel Ministries, 1987).

9. This may be verified by studying Gleason L. Archer and Gregory Chirichigno, *Old Testament Quotations in the New Testament* (Chicago: Moody Press, 1983).

10. *Divine Name*, 23.

11. Ibid., 24.

12. Ibid., 27.

13. On this matter see Mason, *JEHOVAH*.

14. *Divine Name*, 14.

15. Ibid., 15.

16. Ibid., 16.

17. Tryggve N. D. Mettinger, *In Search of God: The Meaning and Message of the Everlasting Names*, trans. Frederick H. Cryer (Philadelphia: Fortress Press, 1988), 15, 209 (n. 2).

18. Ibid., 17.

19. *The Watchtower* 96, 6 (March 15, 1975), 174.

20. Bruce R. McConkie, *A New Witness for the Articles of Faith* (Salt Lake City: Deseret Book Co., 1985), 59–69.

21. On John 1:1 and 20:28, see Bowman, *Jehovah's Witnesses, Jesus Christ, and the Gospel of John*, 17–84, 133–34.

22. DeLacey, "'One Lord' in Pauline Christology," in *Christ the Lord*, 191–203.

23. George Howard, "The Tetragram and the New Testament," *Journal of Biblical Literature* 96 (1977):63–83.

Appendix A: *What Scholars Think of the New World Translation*

1. "How Knowing Greek Led Me to Know God," as told by Nicholas Kip, *Awake!* (March 22, 1987), 12.

2. Ibid., 14.

3. *The Watchtower* (Sept. 1, 1952), 541.

4. William I. Cetnar, *Questions for Jehovah's Witnesses* (Kunkletown, Penn.: W. I. Cetnar, 1983), 69.

5. Alexander Thomson, in *The Differentiator* (April 1952), 52–57, cited in *Awake!* (March 22, 1987), 14. Unfortunately, I still have not been able to track down copies of *The Differentiator*. Enough information exists, however, to make a preliminary evaluation of his comments.

6. Cetnar, *Questions*, 53.

7. Alexander Thomson, in *The Differentiator* (June 1959), cited in Ian Croft, "The New World Translation of the Holy Scriptures: Does It Really Have the Support of Greek Scholars?" (Perth, Western Australia: Concerned Growth Ministries, 1987), 2.

8. Robert M. McCoy, "Jehovah's Witnesses and Their New Testament," *Andover Newton Quarterly* (Jan. 1963), 31.

9. Ibid., 16 note.

10. Ibid., 24.

11. Ibid., 29.

12. William A. Irwin, "Method and Procedure of the Revision," *An Introduction to the Revised Standard Version of the Old Testament* (Chicago: International Council of Religious Education, 1952), 14, cited in McCoy, 29.

13. S. MacLean Gilmour, "The Use and Abuse of the Book of Revelation," *Andover Newton Quarterly* (Sept. 1966), 25–26.

14. Ibid., 16 note.

15. Croft, "New World Translation," 4.

16. Thomas N. Winter, "The Kingdom Interlinear Translation of the Greek Scriptures" (review), *The Classical Journal* (April-May 1974), 376.

17. *Aid to Bible Understanding*, 693, 694.

18. Winter, "Kingdom Interlinear Translation," 375–76.

19. Alfred Marshall (tr.), *Interlinear Greek–English New Testament* (Grand Rapids: Zondervan Publishing House, 1976 reprint).

20. Winter, "Kingdom Interlinear Translation," 376.

21. D. W. Jayne, "Magi," in *Zondervan Pictorial Encyclopedia of the Bible*, Vol. 4 (Grand Rapids: Zondervan Publishing House, 1976), 31–34.

22. David Alexander and Pat Alexander (eds.), *Eerdmans' Handbook to the Bible* (Grand Rapids: William B. Eerdmans Publishing Co., 1973), 79.

23. "Questions from Readers," *The Watchtower* (Feb. 1, 1963), 95.

24. Ernest Cadman Colwell, *What Is the Best New Testament?* (Chicago: University of Chicago Press, 1952), 85.

25. The principal members of the NWT translation committee were Nathan Knorr, then president of the Watchtower Society, and Frederick Franz, the present president and the chief theologian of the Witnesses for decades. Also on the committee were George Gangas and Albert Schroeder. That these men were on the committee has been revealed by former workers at the headquarters in Brooklyn, including Raymond Franz, Frederick Franz's nephew and a former member of the Governing Body. According to Raymond Franz, only Fred Franz had "sufficient knowledge of the Bible languages to attempt translation of this kind. He had studied Greek for two years in the University of Cincinnati but was only self taught in Hebrew." Raymond Franz, *Crisis of Conscience* (Atlanta: Commentary Press, 1983), 50. As M. James Penton, a former Jehovah's Witness and historian, has written, "to all intents and purposes the New World Translation is the work of one man—Frederick Franz." M. James Penton, *Apocalypse Delayed: The Story of Jehovah's Witnesses* (Toronto: University of Toronto Press, 1985), 174.

26. Colwell, 86.

27. Bruce M. Metzger, "Jehovah's Witnesses and Jesus Christ," *Theology Today* (April 1953), 74; see also Metzger, "The New World Translation of the Christian Greek Scriptures," *The Bible Translator* (July 1964).

28. H. H. Rowley, "How Not to Translate the Bible," *The Expository Times* (Nov. 1953), 41–42.

29. Ibid., 42.

30. H. H. Rowley, "Jehovah's Witnesses' Translation of the Bible," *The Expository Times* (Jan. 1956), 106, 107.

Appendix B: *Word Study: Cross or Stake?*

1. See especially (in order of increasing difficulty) James W. Sire, *Scripture Twisting: 20 Ways the Cults Misread the Bible* (Downers Grove, Ill.: InterVarsity Press, 1980); D. A. Carson, *Exegetical Fallacies* (Grand Rapids: Baker Book House, 1984); and Moises Silva, *Biblical Words and Their Meaning: An Introduction to Lexical Semantics* (Grand Rapids: Zondervan Publishing House, 1983).

2. Silva, *Biblical Words*, 104–5.

3. Ibid., 104.

4. Kip, "How Knowing Greek Led Me to Know God," 11.

5. Ibid, 12.

6. *Reasoning from the Scriptures* (WTBTS, 1985), 89.

7. See, for example, D. G. Burke, "Cross; Crucify," *International Standard Bible Encyclopedia*, genl. ed. Geoffrey W. Bromiley, Vol. 1 (Grand Rapids: William B. Eerdmans Publishing Co., 1979), 825–30; and Martin Hengel, *Crucifixion in the Ancient World and the Folly of the Message of the Cross* (Philadelphia: Fortress Press, 1977).

8. E.g., *Reasoning from the Scriptures*, 89–91.

Recommended Reading

This book is intended as an introductory work, and is designed to orient the reader to understand and evaluate the interpretations of the Bible adhered to by Jehovah's Witnesses. I encourage readers to go on to read other books which will help them go deeper into various specific matters relating to this broad subject.

Books about Jehovah's Witnesses

These are some of the best and most recent books about Jehovah's Witnesses which contribute significantly to an understanding of the way they approach the Bible, including but not limited to critiques of their specific interpretations.

Bowman, Robert M., Jr. *Jehovah's Witnesses, Jesus Christ, and the Gospel of John* (Grand Rapids: Baker Book House, 1989).

A thorough refutation of the Jehovah's Witnesses' treatment of John 1:1 and John 8:58, with an appendix on John 20:28. The author invited the Watchtower Society and several Witnesses to write a rebuttal of the book to be included as an appendix, but no one responded to this invitation.

————. *Why You Should Believe in the Trinity: An Answer to Jehovah's Witnesses* (Grand Rapids: Baker Book House, 1989).

A thorough, point-by-point response to the arguments against the Trinity raised in the Watchtower publication *Should You Believe in the Trinity?* (WTBTS, 1989).

Franz, Raymond. *Crisis of Conscience* (Atlanta: Commentary Press, 1984).

A former member of the Governing Body tells why he and many faithful Witnesses were disfellowshiped in the wake of doctrinal and organizational problems in the late 1970s. The book is especially valuable for the insight it gives into how the Governing Body decides what interpretations of the Bible to adopt and how they are written and published.

Jonsson, Carl Olof. *The Gentile Times Reconsidered* (La Jolla, Calif.: Good News Defenders, 1983).

Jonsson, a Swedish Jehovah's Witness elder, set out to prove the Watchtower chronology and interpretation of the Gentile Times right, ended up proving them wrong. After waiting years for the Governing Body to explain his "error," he shared his views and was disfellowshiped.

Magnani, Duane. *The Heavenly Weather Man* (Clayton, Calif.: Witness Inc., 1985).

The title refers to the Jehovah's Witness view of God as a finite being who does not know everything; demonstrates clearly that the God of the Jehovah's Witnesses is not the God of the Bible.

_____. *Point/Counterpoint: A Refutation of the Jehovah's Witness Book **Reasoning from the Scriptures***; Vol. One: *False Prophets* (Clayton, Calif.: Witness Inc., 1986).

A point-by-point refutation of the section on "False Prophets" in *Reasoning from the Scriptures*, using other Watchtower publications to show that the Jehovah's Witnesses cannot escape the charge of false prophecy.

_____, and Arthur Barrett. *Dialogue with Jehovah's Witnesses*, 2 Vols. (Clayton, Calif.: Witness Inc., 1983).

Some dialogues with JWs, with photocopies from their own literature documenting points likely to be challenged. The best of its kind. Published in abridged form as *The Watchtower Files: Dialogue with a Jehovah's Witness* (Minneapolis: Bethany House Publishers, 1985).

_____. *From Kingdom Hall to Kingdom Come*, 2d ed. (Clayton, Calif.: Witness Inc., 1987).

How to lead a Jehovah's Witness to belief in Jesus as risen bodily and as the Lord (Rom. 10:9–10), with lengthy sections on accepting Christ and leaving the Jehovah's Witness organization, and two lengthy appendices on 1 Corinthians 15:44–45. A very useful work.

Mason, Doug. *JEHOVAH in the Jehovah's Witnesses' New World Translation* (Manhattan Beach, Calif.: Bethel Ministries, 1987).

The best critique of the use of *Jehovah* in the Christian Greek Scriptures (New Testament) of the NWT, focusing on textual evidences.

Penton, M. James. *Apocalypse Delayed: The Story of Jehovah's Witnesses* (Toronto: University of Toronto Press, 1985).

A Canadian Jehovah's Witness historian, whose previous work was lauded by the Witnesses, set out to write a complete history of the Jehovah's Witnesses. His findings led to his being disfellowshiped. The book, which is the best history of the Jehovah's Witnesses to date, reflects the point of view of a nonevangelical ex-Jehovah's Witness. It is most helpful in understanding the social and intellectual background and development of Jehovah's Witness thought, and most unhelpful when Penton voices his own opinions on fine points of biblical interpretation.

Reed, David A. *Answering Jehovah's Witnesses Verse by Verse* (Grand Rapids: Baker Book House, 1987).

Arranged in biblical order from Genesis to Revelation, this book contains answers to Jehovah's Witness misuse of Scripture found nowhere else.

_____. *How to Rescue Your Loved One from the Watchtower* (Grand Rapids: Baker Book House, 1989).

Perhaps the best introductory book on Jehovah's Witnesses for someone who wants to help a friend or relative out of the Jehovah's Witnesses.

Watters, Randall. *Refuting Jehovah's Witnesses* (Manhattan Beach, Calif.: Bethel Ministries, 1987).

A comprehensive critique of Jehovah's Witness teachings, covering most of the same material and organized in similar fashion to the Watchtower book *Reasoning from the Scriptures* (WTBTS, 1985) from the point of view of an evangelical ex-Jehovah's Witness.

Evangelical Books on Biblical Interpretation

It is not enough to learn how Jehovah's Witnesses read the Bible incorrectly; one must go on to learn how to do it correctly. There are an enormous number of excellent books in this area (as well as a large number of less helpful and of extremely poor books). The following are just a sample. Reading some of these books should go a long way toward helping the Jehovah's Witness see that the real Bible students of the world are evangelicals.

Archer, Gleason L. *Encyclopedia of Bible Difficulties* (Grand Rapids: Zondervan Publishing House, 1982).

A reference work arranged from Genesis to Revelation, to be dipped into rather than read straight through; answers apparent contradictions, defends the historical and scientific accuracy of the Bible, and much more.

Carson, D. A. *Exegetical Fallacies* (Grand Rapids: Baker Book House, 1984).

A moderately advanced work on biblical interpretation focusing on mistakes even sophisticated evangelicals make in their interpretations of the Bible. Carson even points out a couple of mistakes he made in the past! This book does at least two things relevant to us: it teaches Bible students how to avoid various common mistakes (some of which the Jehovah's Witnesses commit in their publication); and it exemplifies the fact that evangelicals generally recognize that their interpretations are fallible and work hard to learn from each other and from their own mistakes.

Frame, John M. *The Doctrine of the Knowledge of God: A Theology of Lordship* (Grand Rapids: Baker Book House, 1988).

An advanced study of what it means to know God, and how we know God and learn his truth from the Bible.

Gaffin, Richard B., Jr. *Resurrection and Redemption: A Study in Paul's Soteriology*, rev. ed. (Grand Rapids: Baker Book House, 1988).

A model example of Bible study, and incidentally very helpful for understanding the true significance of Jesus' resurrection.

Geisler, Norman L., and William E. Nix. *A General Introduction to the Bible*, rev. ed. (Chicago: Moody Press, 1986).

The history of the Bible from original manuscripts to twentieth-century translations; a masterful reference work.

Hoekema, Anthony A. *The Bible and the Future* (Grand Rapids: William B. Eerdmans Publishing Co., 1979).

One of the very best evangelical textbooks on such subjects as future prophecy, the kingdom of God, the Millennium, heaven, hell, and the new earth (yes, at least some evangelicals believe in the new earth).

Morris, Leon. *The Apostolic Preaching of the Cross*, 3d ed. (Grand Rapids: William B. Eerdmans Publishing Co., 1965).

A classic work examining the biblical teaching on the significance of Christ's death.

Packer, James I. *Knowing God* (Downers Grove, Ill.: InterVarsity Press, 1973).

One of the most popular evangelical books, and rightly so; should be very helpful in reorienting a Jehovah's Witness to appreciate what being a Christian is all about.

Poythress, Vern S. *Symphonic Theology: The Validity of Multiple Perspectives in Theology* (Grand Rapids: Zondervan Publishing House—Academie Books, 1987).

Truth is absolute, but human perspectives on truth are not, argues Poythress. A single perspective can even be completely true without being the whole story. Thus, we can learn from truth that others see, and use that truth to help them see the truth they have missed. How can we appreciate the genuine insights into the Bible that Jehovah's Witnesses do have while we show that their views are basically unbiblical? This book provides an answer.

Reymond, Robert L. *Jesus, Divine Messiah: The New Testament Witness* (Phillipsburg, N.J.: Presbyterian & Reformed Publishing Co., 1990).

A comprehensive, thorough defense of the deity of Christ, focusing on denials of Christ's deity by liberal Protestants.

Sproul, R. C. *Knowing Scripture* (Downers Grove, Ill.: InterVarsity Press, 1973).

One of the best short introductions to proper methods of reading the Bible.

For Further Information

To obtain helpful literature, receive answers to questions, or meet people who are able to give valuable support to Jehovah's Witnesses who are rethinking their beliefs, please contact the following organizations:

Bethel Ministries
P. O. Box 3818
Manhattan Beach, CA 90266
(213) 545–7831

Provides help in all areas and especially assists ex-Witnesses to find fellowship and grow as Christians.

Christian Research Institute
P. O. Box 500
San Juan Capistrano, CA
92693–0500
(714) 855–9926

Covers a wide range of issues besides Jehovah's Witnesses; especially strong in the areas of biblical interpretation and Christian doctrine.

Comments from the Friends
P. O. Box 840
Stoughton, MA 02072
(617) 584–4467

Provides help in all areas and especially assists those who are still Witnesses but are searching for truth.

Personal Freedom Outreach
P. O. Box 26062
St. Louis, MO 63136
(314) 388–2684

Provides help in all areas and especially equips Christians to evangelize Jehovah's Witnesses and persons of other unorthodox beliefs.

Witness Inc.
P. O. Box 597
Clayton, CA 94517
(415) 672-5979

Provides help in all areas and especially offers documentation exposing the false teachings, false prophecies, and authoritarianism of the Watchtower.

Subject Index

Scripture Index

Note: The following texts are not indexed: (a) those using the expression "Amen I say to you" listed on page 100; (b) those in which the NWT has Jesus using the name *Jehovah,* listed on page 117. Page numbers where the biblical text is discussed in some depth are italicized.

163